# CONFLICT

*Turning a Life of Work*
*into a Work of Art*

## A TOUCHSTONE BOOK

Published by Simon & Schuster Inc.

NEW YORK · LONDON · TORONTO · SYDNEY · TOKYO

*This book is dedicated to those who suspect that*
*there is more to life than they are presently experiencing*
*and are willing to enter into the unknown to claim it.*

**Touchstone**
Simon & Schuster Building
Rockefeller Center
1230 Avenue of the Americas
New York, New York 10020

Copyright © 1987 by Thomas Crum
All rights reserved
including the right of reproduction
in whole or in part in any form
First Touchstone Edition, 1988
TOUCHSTONE and colophon are registered trademarks of
Simon & Schuster Inc.
Designed by Eve Kirch
Manufactured in the United States of America

10  9  8  7  6  5  4  3  2  1

10  9  8  7  6  5  4  3  2      Pbk.

Library of Congress Cataloging in Publication Data
Crum, Thomas F.
   The magic of conflict.
   Bibliography: p.
   1. Interpersonal conflict.   2. Conflict (Psychology)
3. Aikido—Psychological aspects.   I. Title.
BF637.I48C78   1987      158'.2      87-9691
ISBN 0-671-63818-1
ISBN 0-671-66836-6 Pbk.

*The author is grateful for permission to reprint material from the following:*
   *Critical Path* by R. Buckminster Fuller. Copyright © 1981 by R. Buckminster Fuller.
St. Martin's Press, 1981. Used by permission.
   "The Secret Sits" by Robert Frost. Copyright © 1969 by Holt, Rinehart & Winston, Inc.
Copyright 1942 by Robert Frost. Copyright © 1970 by Lesley Frost Ballantine. Reprinted
from *The Poetry of Robert Frost,* edited by Edward Connery Latham, by permission of
Henry Holt and Company, Inc.

*(Continued on p. 254)*

# THE MAGIC OF

## OF

# Thomas F. Crum

Foreword by John Denver
Photographs by John Denver and Doug Child
Illustrations by Tammie Lane

# CONTENTS

# ACKNOWLEDGMENTS

I'd like to make a toast to all those people who have made a difference in my life, and as a result have contributed—in one way or another—to the shaping of this book. You know who you are. You are the ones who told me the truth even when it was uncomfortable. You are the ones who, through your coaching, your listening, your inspirational models and support, helped me clarify my thoughts and focus my vision.

A toast to Barbara Heckendorn, whose dedication and willingness to do whatever it takes has been a source of support to me since word one.

To Richard Compton, who helped with the last drafts of this book. His writing and thinking skills brought it to a new level of clarity and quality.

To photographer Doug Child and his wife, Suzanne, for their artistry.

To my friend and agent, Jan Miller, and to Editor Bob Asahina and his staff for their confidence in me.

To Chrissy Gibbs and Judy Warner for their ideas, time, and support.

To my Aiki assistant, Tom Eckstein, whose clear thinking, loyalty, and commitment to the Aiki Approach has been a true source of strength and friendship.

To all my students, workshop participants, and friends who share in the Aiki work/play, giving honest suggestions and lots of enthusiasm.

A toast to Windstar, its staff and members, for the opportunity to serve and be served.

To my martial arts teachers, friends, and colleagues: Morihei Ueshiba, Koichi Tohei, Rod Kobayashi, Bob Bishop, Richard Bustillo, Clarence Chinn, John Clodig, Terry Dobson, Bob Duggan, Al Huang, Marshall Ho'o, Dan Inosanto, Harry Ishasaka, George Leonard, Walt Muryasz, Clayton Naluai, Minoru Oshima, David Shaner, Jon Takagi, and Mitz Yamashada.

A special toast to many supporters, nurturers, and inspirations: Michael Abdo, Nan and Fouad Azzam, Peggy and Donald Abell, Russell Bishop and the "Insight" group, Ken and Marge Blanchard, Bill Browning, Cheryl Charles, Ashley and Doss Carrithers, Diane Cirincione, Linda and Steve Conger, Richard Diehl, Werner Erhard, Bill Farley, Bucky Fuller, Tim Gallwey, and Bruce Gordon.

To John Graham, Susan Greene, Herb Hamsher, Willis Harman, Terry Hubka, Arthur Jackson, Jerry Jampolsky, Spencer Johnson, Elisa Julien, Dawn Kairns, John Katzenberger, Larry Kendall, Randy Kunkel, Richard Lamm, Tammie Lane, the Leary family, Jim Laue, Amory and Hunter Lovins, Maharishi Mahesh Yogi, Ann Medlock, W. Mitchell, Bev Moore, David Neenan, Richard Noffsinger, Klaus Obermeyer, Rod O'Connor, John Phillips, Vince Pugliese, Chuck Racine, Ram Dass, Dave Randle, Tony and Becky Robbins, Bob Samples, Rusty Schweickart, Ellen Stapenhorst, Ray Schonholtz, David Spangler, Kollene Sublette, Hal and Dorothy Thau, Bill Thistle, Marshall Thurber, Tom Vondruska, Ian and Vicky Watson, Treya and Ken Wilbur, Wyatt Woodsmall, the members of the Alive Tribe, Buckminster Fuller Institute, and The World Game, Inc.

To my parents, Tom and Lucille Crum, who have always been there for me with total love and support.

To Cathy and our children, Tommy, Eri, and Ali, who have been my greatest teachers and closest friends.

And especially to John Denver, who is like a brother to me—the best kind of brother, the one you can count on when the chips are down. Thank you, John—and all of you—for all that you have given to me.

# FOREWORD

When Tom Crum and I began working together, I knew I had found a true ally, someone who could help me put my feelings into practice. For all of my life I have abhorred violence. When I was a child, I would walk away from a fight, even at the risk of being called "chicken." My fear was that I would hurt someone. My faith was that there were other ways to take a stand: ways that would strengthen a relationship, not break it down; ways that would prove a point, not negate it; ways that would demonstrate the value of a position and not diminish it through violence. Being stronger or tougher or meaner didn't make that someone right. As far as I was concerned, resorting to violence, more often than not, was proof of a person's self-doubt and insecurity, not their strength. It demonstrated not a lack of intelligence, but a lack of consciousness. And to me, that is just what the resolution of conflict is all about. Consciousness. It is what moving beyond success is all about. Inner and outer peace—as a conscious choice.

It is not always a simple, obvious, or easy choice. The tendency toward fighting is deeply ingrained in our thoughts and feelings and it takes personal commitment and a genuine understanding of the alternatives to turn it around.

In this book, Tom shares his discoveries in the art of conflict resolution, gained, in part, through many years of studying and teaching the martial arts. Tom's teaching goes beyond the traditional combative forms to show how the power of harmony and love can work in even the most difficult of situations.

Tom continues to be, for me, the best example of a commitment to peace through his work in the creative resolution of conflict. Over the years, Tom has been the one that I turned to when I was immersed in my own struggles and unable to see my own life clearly. He brings me back to center, to where the real clarity unfolds, to conscious listening—within and without. More importantly, he practices what he preaches. In this book, he has articulated powerful and effective options for dealing with conflict and for moving beyond mere success. It is what it takes to be truly human.

The choices that Tom reveals don't stop at a personal or business level. We can make a conscious choice about nuclear weapons in the world and defense spending when we can understand not only what it is costing us in every aspect of our lives, but its relationship to the deep, unresolved struggles within ourselves. And, just as importantly, what the alternatives to struggle are and how they respond to the most profound questions we can ask ourselves about humanity and its place in the universe.

This is a critical time in the history of life on the planet earth. Decisions are being made and actions taken which are going to affect not only our lives, but those of all future generations, and, in fact, the potential for life itself on our beautiful Spaceship Earth. It is of the utmost importance that whatever decisions are made, whatever actions taken, they be a reflection of the hearts of *all* who make up the family of humankind on this planet and, even more importantly, the product of our ever-expanding consciousness.

The Aiki Approach that Thomas Crum articulates in this book really *works*. Tom takes us simply, clearly, and profoundly through the nature of conflict and the principles of the Aiki Approach for resolving conflict and moving beyond success, and provides us with real, practical applications of these principles to our daily life. These principles work on an individual level, in the simplest of relationships, and in the most complex, even those between societies and nations which espouse differences in language, heritage, politics, and faith. Transformation takes risk and courage. This book provides you with real support for both.

This is no longer a world of you *or* me. We must recognize that it is you *and* me and that together we can create the world, the life that we have dreamed of forever, a world of peace and goodwill among men. A world without hunger. A world without the threat of a nuclear disaster and the possible extinction of humanity. Peace *is* a conscious choice.

John Denver

# INTRODUCTION

Success is such an enticing word. Triumph, achievement, and winning have always been among our great motivators. This book is for those who want to go beyond success.

When we take a long, deep look at those gold medals we have achieved in life, whether they be titles and recognition, jobs, material wealth, or relationships, we often recognize that something is missing. It is difficult to place our finger on this gnawing lack of fulfillment. Successes do not fill every moment. Life is still full of upsets, frustrations, emptiness, and irritability. This is the point of conflict when what we get in life doesn't match up with what we thought we wanted. In our insatiable quest for more medals and more social acknowledgments, we accept mediocrity, or worse, in terms of personal fulfillment and happiness. We accept the absence of disease to be health. We accept just getting along with another to be a decent relationship. Even if we are fortunate enough to reach the heights of success by societal standards, the lack of fulfillment often remains.

What does it take to break out of this pattern? Is it possible to move *beyond* success, to turn frustration into fascination, upset into joy, and our busy-ness into well-being? To do this we need to make a shift in our ability to deal with the many conflicts in our lives, to make our conflicts into opportunities—literally, the best opportunities we have to grow, to learn, and to create. Often this requires a courageous leap into a whole new perception of relationships.

Conflict has been our daily companion since childhood. Do you remember the struggle of trying to tie your shoes (or even find them) while the "big" kids were already going off to play, or that horrible sound of *splat!* as your newly bought ice cream cone hit the pavement after only two licks? Or the disappointment of not being big enough to ride the roller coaster? Or the anxious moments dashing by the neighbor's house where the ferocious dog inevitably lurked? Although our early childhood was often blissful, those daily stumbles and spilt milk bumbles still spring up in our minds as part of growing up.

As we reached school age, those conflicts did not leave, they only changed their form. How do I look? Do you think she likes me? Do my friends think I'm OK? Will I pass that test? When will vacation begin? How much can I get away with tonight without getting caught? These were the hidden curricula of each school year.

Does any of this sound familiar? What is extraordinary about these daily conflicts is the vast amount of learning that occurs as we work through them. And what is even more remarkable is that we are, for the most part, ignorant of the great value of this process. In the midst of this most splendid opportunity for growing and learning that we call conflict, we spend our time grumbling, complaining, and justifying. When we see conflict as the enemy, we tend to use much of our immense brain-power and energy avoiding it, denying it, or fighting it. We have accepted this reaction to conflict just as we have accepted—hook, line, and sinker—most of the other cultural and societal norms around us. In growing up, there was a constant pull to obey every "you should do this" and "you should do that," to do what was acceptable so that we would be accepted in turn. We were unaware of the subtle hypnotic trance in which we were operating, robotically accepting things as "The Way It Is," seldom venturing inside our own being to discover our true feelings, emotions, and needs. The desire to leap into the unknown was usually considered dangerously foolish at best.

The words "Sit still!" and "Don't rock back in your chair" grated at us daily in the classroom. Even if we knew intuitively that movement and learning somehow went together, we would hold our bodies still and the open door to our minds would become partially closed in the process.

"Eat everything on your plate" is another phrase with which people are still struggling—witness the constant dieting around you. When we did uncover an emotion or desire that was in conflict with the norms of society, it was easy to be bullied back into line with admonishments such as "What do you know? You're just a kid," or "Straighten up and fly right."

Most of us have experienced a strong dose of this societal pressure. I was no different. The need for approval—from my parents, my teachers, and my friends—motivated me to successfully complete the cultural indoctrination of my youth. By my senior year in college, I was another typical American success-story unfolding—a basically healthy, athletic, and popular young guy preparing to graduate with honors and a degree in mathematics and education.

Meanwhile, the pressure inside was building. I was continually denying or resisting the conflict in my life. As the buildup of pressure continued, eventually it had to find an outlet. The universe provides us with a marvelous ability to grow and to change, whether we want to or not. In my case, I let the pressure build up enough so that my body literally broke down. An excellent athlete all my life and a starting collegiate football player, I found myself in the hospital with back and knee injuries so serious that when I awoke from a four-hour operation and asked the doctor when I'd be able to play football again, the doctor calmly declared, "You won't be doing anything more active than walking. That knee is finished."

When I visited another doctor, I was cautioned to limit myself for the rest of my life to mild exercise such as golf. Suddenly, I had created a far more challenging script with which to deal. I was forced to take a deep breath and look inside. Did I have to submit to that destiny or did I have a choice? And what had caused the rug to be so abruptly pulled out from under my dancing feet?

Isn't it interesting how, during crises, we consider our own problems as "real" tragedies, as if we carry a bigger weight on our shoulders than the next guy? And then, to prove how tragic our lives are, we create more difficulties. Not only did I do a great job of creating havoc in my body, but my emotional and mental bubble burst soon thereafter. My girlfriend became pregnant and the big *R* of responsibility became indelibly planted on my consciousness. Add to this the pressure to use that "education" of mine to provide a decent living for my new family. I created a job I disliked but which made everyone around me happy because of my "mature attitude," and placed myself in a big city environment that a mountain boy like myself would usually turn away from, given half a chance. In hindsight, as I write this, all these "difficulties" seem trivial, but at the time I felt they were tragic.

Now, this is the stuff that makes soap operas interesting. I felt I had become physically damaged, burdened with responsibility and a frustrating job that I disliked, and a dweller in an environment not of my choosing. Does any of this sound familiar?

Is it possible that we have been so hypnotized by our cultural indoctrination over the years that we see nothing but what we *should* do, interpreting that as the only thing we *can* do? And do we see the rest of our lives as offering simply more of the same, with the probable exception of things getting worse?

As Woody Allen put it, "More than at any other time in history mankind faces a crossroads. One path leads to despair and utter hopelessness; the other to total extinction. Let us pray we have the wisdom to choose correctly." [1]

Having hit rock bottom in my despair, an odd thought crossed my mind. Was this some form of slow suicide that I'd created, some unconscious desire to die? If that were true, I thought, why didn't I have the courage to really jump? Then I started thinking: If I was going to jump, why not do it more elegantly than the sidewalk splatter and bridge droppings you hear about? Why not truly jump—leap fully into life, giving myself to the world? Why hold back? What was I risking, considering the quality of experience I was having then? I thought, "go ahead and jump."

The first leap was to tell myself the truth and begin to listen to and follow my heart. Suddenly the boundaries that had looked so insurmountable developed a window, or at least a hole, through which a breath of fresh air found its way. By making a conscious choice, that opening became a doorway to understanding and opportunity. And in my strong desire to open wide this doorway of my life, I have discovered ways which help me to effortlessly remove the entire boundary. Frustration is turning into fascination and upset into growth. More and more I seem to be exactly where I want to be, doing what I want to do. My work is my play and my play is my work. The purpose of this book is to share my discovery, which I call the Aiki Approach, with you.

The daily struggles and conflicts are still there. It is our relationship to them that can be totally different. Instead of seeing the rug being pulled out from under us, we can learn to dance on a shifting carpet. The stumbling blocks of the past magically become the stepping stones to the future. The walls and boundaries of old can offer interesting vistas as we move beyond them.

Thomas F. Crum

# THE CHALLENGE

To see a World in a Grain of Sand
And a Heaven in a Wildflower
Hold Infinity in the palm of your hand
And Eternity in an hour.

William Blake

# 1. The Extraordinary State

Humans are such a magical lot. Over time, even our wildest dreams can become realities. Consider flying. Since the earliest times, man has longed to soar with the birds, looking down on the whole world from a place of heavenly freedom. Today we can soar and glide and swoop with the best of our fine-feathered friends. And we can do it all with no effort, freeing us to be fully conscious of the experience.

And yet, man is a curious species. Having realized his grandest dreams, he immediately forgets to enjoy them. With a peculiar flair, he can turn the glory of flight into just one more modern convenience. As he rushes down the concourse, burdened with a briefcase and over-stuffed hanging bag, he grimly loosens his tie for the final sprint to the gate. He glances at the clock. One minute to go.

Sweat begins to bead on his face as he breaks into a run, pushing obliviously through the splendor of humanity around him. Waving his boarding pass at the sweetly smiling stewardess, he limps onto the plane and flops, exhausted, into his seat.

"Tough day?" I inquire.

"They're all tough," he says, surprised to find someone sitting next to him. Then he relaxes, letting his breath out all the way. "Oh well, at least it's over."

"Was it at least successful?" I probe, hopefully.

"Yeah, I guess it was," he says, hardly noticing as the silvery winged bird taxis us toward the runway. "I feel beat-up and can't wait to get home so I can get some rest and get my health back together." He looks tired, but not with that euphoric kind of tiredness that you get from a good workout or a satisfying day's work. He is oblivious to the fact that we are about to lift off the ground and experience a miracle never thought possible until less than a century ago.

"It just doesn't seem fair, does it?" he adds wryly. "You work your tail off all week to get what you want and then you're too tired to enjoy it. Sometimes I wonder whether it's really worth it." Totally unaware of our eagle's view of the brilliantly colored planet, we move through the heavens, approaching the speed of sound.

"Basically, when I think about it, my life has been successful. I've accomplished a lot," he says, talking as much to himself as to me. "Yet, when I have a moment like this to really take a good hard look, I'm still not there. I get upset and irritated with everyone, including myself. Then I get so caught up in my work. I'll miss a whole day sometimes, I'll get so occupied with what I'm doing."

He pauses for a long thoughtful moment.

"It's just that I'm way too busy! There's never enough time to do what *I* want to do. If I could just stop long enough to figure a way out of this rat race, I'd be all right."

So much for the glory of flight.

It's such a cliche—the stressed-out businessman, the "mid-life crisis." Yet it touches the pulse of our entire culture, diagnosing a general malaise of modern life.

In this electronic jet-age world, it is easy to feel as if you're trapped on a merry-go-round of activity that keeps increasing in speed and complexity, and the longer you stay on the less chance there is of getting off. Is it possible to enjoy the passing scenery from this runaway freight train we have created?

Often in life we win those "gold medals" that we are striving for —in business, the arts, sports, or relationships. Yet in our quietest moments we recognize that success alone does not provide fulfillment. Something is lacking; the taste of success is there only momentarily, like your favorite cookie. Once you've eaten it, you're looking around for one more bite, one more cookie. The craving hasn't subsided. The contentment is elusive. The struggle for the next job, relationship, or possession begins again, along with all the feelings of insecurity and anxiety.

The question that I would put to my hypothetical friend in the airplane, that I am going to put to you, is: What would it be like if we lived our lives as works of art in progress? What would it be like if we could live joyfully in every moment, absorbing the magic and freshness of each new day without hurry? What would it be like if each breath and each action were part of an unfolding masterpiece, a continued process of artistry? Is this possible?

We experienced artistry when we were children—wide-eyed, discovering, and magical, with all our senses alive. Most of us have also briefly experienced this realm since growing out of childhood, in those exciting moments of falling in love, those exhilarating accomplishments on the sporting field, or the creative light of new ideas suddenly shining through us in the office, at home, or even while driving in rush hour traffic. It's easy to visualize the possibilities of living a life of artistry when everything is going well.

But what happens when conflict arises, when our lover turns away, when we stumble and drop the ball, when our employer sits us down for a "talk"? Then our depth of character reveals itself. We tend to react unconsciously to pressure and the unexpected in ways that we have developed from our past experiences and from observing what is around us—our parents, our friends, the movies, or the TV set. Since so often what we observe in crises is people in struggle, pain, and fear, is it any wonder that our ordinary reaction becomes a confused combination of those elements?

There *is* an alternative. This book will provide the reader with a way of responding to crises that is extraordinary. Integrating this approach will enable you to bring forth a life of power, freedom, and joy. Using pressure, change, and the unknown, an artist can sculpt a masterpiece. Seeing conflict as an opportunity to create art from our very being is a challenge for the artist in all of us.

Our lives are not dependent on whether or not we have conflict. It is what we *do* with conflict that makes the difference.

\* \* \*

If we take a moment to examine our typical reactions to life's experiences, we will find that they usually fall into one of five general mind-sets:

## Survival

One of the most common reactions is that of survival. When we perceive ourselves as separate and disconnected from those around us, there comes a feeling of "you or me" and a sense that there isn't enough for both of us. This perception of scarcity develops a mind-set of survival, and people today spend a significant portion of their time operating in this mode. We fear that there is not enough money, energy, or resources to go around. Therefore the tendency is to get all we can for us and ours and to keep the doors barred and the guns cocked because somebody's always trying to get at the cookie jar. Survival manifests itself daily in attitudes like the following:

"I'm just getting by, just staying afloat."
"I never have enough time."
"I'm just hanging on to my relationship with my spouse and kids."
"I seem to have to work harder and harder to keep my body healthy. It seems like every time I turn around I'm going to a doctor or a dentist."
"I have to stay on my toes all the time."

In the scarcity context, the experience is one of tremendous energy output, but the net result is mere survival. Like swimming in a strong current, all of our energy seems to be used in maintaining our position or staying afloat.

## Decay

As we become increasingly fatigued from the struggle to survive, we sometimes slip downward into decay and negativity. We perceive everything as going downhill:

"Every year inflation is winning the race with my income. I'm actually losing financial power."

"Just look at this newspaper. The world gets worse every day."

"We hardly ever talk anymore."

"The things these kids are doing these days. It's not like it used to be."

"My body just keeps getting older and slower and fatter."

"Life's a drag and it's pulling me down with it."

*   *   *

There is a net loss of energy in this mode. We are tired and run-down. All action appears pointless. Why do anything?

## Destruction

When we perceive our life as stuck on an inevitable path of continual decay, we tend to label ourselves as a "failure." When we resign ourselves to a life of failure, there is often a desire to pull others down with us. There is a tendency toward total destruction. Certainly we see this in terrorist activities throughout the world, in the killing of our fellow humans, and in the plunder of our planet. This destructive tendency is also very obvious in suicide; it is less obvious but also visible in those in desperate pursuit of health-damaging lifestyles. Destruction can also happen much more subtly, as in people who constantly undermine every activity in order to justify their own deep feelings of inadequacy. The "Yes, but" office worker who always criticizes and sabotages other people's *esprit de corps,* positive attitudes, and new ideas is an excellent case in point. Everyone loses in this "destruct" mode—the person himself, his fellow employees, and the organization. The energy is flowing rapidly on a negative course.

Survival, apathy, and destruction are mind-sets that we have all experienced. They are uncomfortable and damaging to our self-esteem and well-being. There is a continual loss of energy, an increase in fear and separation, and a feeling of struggle and strain. It is no wonder that humans are often in search of a better way of living. However, just as everyone has experienced the feelings of scarcity and apathy, we have also had our moments of success. They can be as unique as winning the Superbowl, or as commonplace as learning to walk, helping a friend in need, or graduating from elementary school.

## Success

In our better moments, we experience our lives as being full of choices and opportunities. We see ourselves as successful and we operate that way. Successful people use conflict as a motivator. They are productive, have lots of energy, and are achieving the gold medals that society holds provocatively in front of them. And yet, within all this activity, there is a sense of "busy-ness" and frenetic energy. It's as if we are always beginning another painting and there are six unfinished ones left at home. The stressful side of this productive mode can be seen in the following:

> "I have a new car, now I need a new sailboat."
> "Sit down while I show you my trophies and talk about all the celebrities I've met."
> "I'd love to spend more time with you, but I'm over my head in work."
> "Once I get this project completed, then I can finally do what I really want to do."

Still, in this mode, we have an abundance of energy; a positive, forward-looking attitude; and a keen awareness of opportunity. It is precisely these attributes that can catapult us beyond success.

## Artistry

To move beyond success is to make our life of work a work of art. We see the world around us as an extension of ourselves. In this state it is natural to support and cooperate with one another. The "I win and you lose" approach in the scarcity model becomes an "I win and you win" prerequisite, in business as well as in personal relationships. We move into this "you *and* me" philosophy naturally because we see the world as abundant and supportive in all aspects of our lives, from our health and our family to our financial well-being. We emerge as the new alchemists of the world, regardless of our professions. (Alchemy is the ability to change the ordinary into the extraordinary.) The alchemy of the middle ages had to do with changing common metals into gold. The alchemy of today has to do with changing ourselves.

Is such a transformation possible? Consider the magic of photosynthesis, where plants take water and carbon dioxide and convert them into oxygen, the life-supplying food for the planet. For this magic to occur, it needs the activator and energy source of *light*.

$$H_2O + CO_2 \xrightarrow{\text{light}} CH_2O + O_2$$

The equation describing the alchemy of changing you is a profound one:

$$Ordinary\ People + Ordinary\ Resources + Ordinary\ Circumstances \xrightarrow{\text{conflict}}$$
$$Extraordinary\ States\ of\ Being + Extraordinary\ Results$$

What is the activator or energy source for transforming the ordinary to the extraordinary? It is the pressure of conflict, the interference patterns of energies caused by differences, that provides the motivation and opportunity for change.

We are all basically ordinary. None of us has more than one brain, is free of the need to take time to eat and breathe, or goes through life without any conflicts. Einstein flunked math, the Wright Brothers were simple bicycle mechanics, and Mark Twain never took a high school English course. What is extraordinary about each of these people is that they chose to respond to life's ordinary conflicts from an extraordinary state of vision and action. It is in this extraordinary state that they produced profound results. The act of producing the results in turn reinforces the extraordinary state. We move on a path of increased energy and decreased effort. We are beyond success.

The graph on page 27 summarizes the five general mind-sets discussed previously. The solid line indicates where we spend most of our time today. The dotted line points to the direction of this book —to shift us fully and dramatically beyond the ordinary. It will provide the living formula for this life-transforming alchemy. As we apply the formula daily, our tendency toward a knee-jerk or unconscious reaction to conflict will be replaced by a conscious response. Freedom, joy, and adding value to our world will become available to us each moment.

Nothing gives us a greater opportunity to break through to "artistry" than conflict. It is precisely this understanding and our ability to capitalize on conflict that will enable us to accomplish all we desire and, in so doing, help us to appreciate and enhance the most precious moment of our life—*this moment.*

---

*In the Orient, there is a story of a samurai who is being chased by a bear. He literally runs off a cliff. As he's falling, he grabs a branch.*

*He looks up and sees the bear leaning over the cliff, clawing at his head, missing only by inches. As he looks down to the ground below, only about fifteen feet, he sees a lion leaping up, missing his feet only by inches. As he looks at the branch he is clutching, he sees two groundhogs gnawing away at it. He watches as his lifeline disappears, bite by bite.*

*As he takes a deep, long breath, he notices, next to his branch, a clump of wild strawberries. In the midst of the clump is a great, red, juicy strawberry. With his one free hand, he reaches over, picks the strawberry, puts it in his mouth, chews it slowly and says, "Ah—delicious."*

---

I know of no human being who has lived a powerful and successful life, a life of vision, commitment, and contribution to the world around him, who has not created crises and turmoil. When we live that fully, it is inevitable that we will encounter those bears of the past, lions of the future, and groundhogs of the present. Major life crises or cumulative daily struggles have the potential to destroy the strongest of us. Yet even in the midst of conflict, it is possible to move beyond, to shift our attention from potential disaster to the sweetness and opportunity of the moment. And it is in choosing to enjoy the present moment that we most effectively create the life we want to live.

**The trouble with the rat race is that even when you win, you're still a rat.**
                                                        Jane Wagner

## HOW WE RESPOND TO CONFLICT*

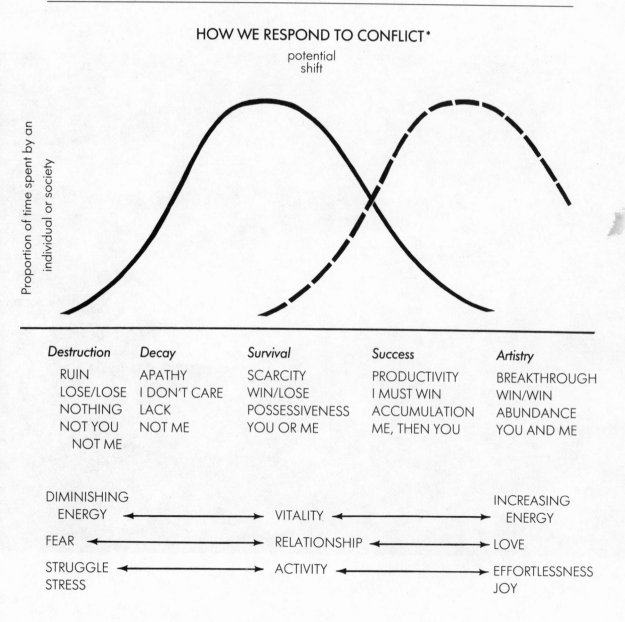

potential
shift

Proportion of time spent by an individual or society

| Destruction | Decay | Survival | Success | Artistry |
|---|---|---|---|---|
| RUIN | APATHY | SCARCITY | PRODUCTIVITY | BREAKTHROUGH |
| LOSE/LOSE | I DON'T CARE | WIN/LOSE | I MUST WIN | WIN/WIN |
| NOTHING | LACK | POSSESSIVENESS | ACCUMULATION | ABUNDANCE |
| NOT YOU | NOT ME | YOU OR ME | ME, THEN YOU | YOU AND ME |
| NOT ME | | | | |

DIMINISHING ENERGY ←——————→ VITALITY ←——————→ INCREASING ENERGY

FEAR ←——————→ RELATIONSHIP ←——————→ LOVE

STRUGGLE STRESS ←——————→ ACTIVITY ←——————→ EFFORTLESSNESS JOY

* Based on research and development by Randy Kunkel, Ph.D., Enterprise, Inc., 202 East Cheyenne Mountain Boulevard, Suite N, Colorado Springs, Colorado 80906. Used with permission.

# 2. The Nature of Conflict

### Conflict.

It appears to be everywhere. We find it in our personal lives at home, between parent and child and between spouses. We find it at work between employer and employee. It's there between man and woman. We see religion against religion, nation against nation. It's the underlying theme throughout all of human history. With the increasing complexity of life on this planet, the exploding human population, and our possession of awesome weapons which could trigger our total annihilation, conflict has become the critical issue of our time.

Where does much of this conflict originate? We certainly don't have to go very far to discover a source. Have you ever closed your eyes for fifteen seconds and monitored the thoughts running through your mind? What a breakneck pace! All that in only fifteen seconds. Given any significant conflict, the conscious mind can easily come up with much more in that time. And the subconscious mind could fill volumes. And consider that there are 5,760 of these fifteen-second intervals in each and every day.

You would think that understanding and handling conflict would be a major priority in our lives. Yet we rarely attempt to understand it. We try to avoid it or we resist it. But it always comes back to haunt us. Have you ever avoided keeping adequate financial records only to find yourself paying for it in time and money at tax time? Or have you ever resisted a healthy exercise or nutrition program only to regret it each time you glance in the mirror? How many times have you avoided telling an uncomfortable truth only to find the problem magnified with time, making the eventual telling much more difficult?

Instead of denying conflict, this book is an invitation to embrace it and to understand it. When we do, it becomes one of the greatest gifts we have for positive growth and change, an empowering and energizing opportunity. There is truly a magical quality about conflict which can call out the best in us, that which is not summoned under ordinary circumstances.

---

*It is said that what the caterpillar calls the end of the world the master calls the butterfly. There is a Zen story about a peasant farmer who owned a beautiful horse desired by others. One day it disappeared. When all the villagers remarked on his bad luck, he calmly replied, "Maybe so, maybe not." A few days later the horse returned, leading a herd of fine wild horses. A week later, his only son was thrown and crippled while training the horses. When the villagers again remarked on his bad luck, he calmly replied, "Maybe so, maybe not." Within a week, a frivolous war was declared by the emperor and all young men, save the farmer's son, were forced into battle and none returned.*

---

Buckminster Fuller[2] was one of the great thinkers of our time. His contributions range from inventions such as the geodesic dome to detailing an entire "critical path" to insure a prosperous future for humanity. He often told us that if we really wanted to understand the principles of the universe, we should look closely at nature. Nature is the ultimate model of success. Bucky was frequently alarmed at the differences between nature's principles and human perceptions. Through a series of misperceptions, man has perpetuated some myths that are very detrimental to the successful resolution of conflict.

One of the myths is the idea that conflict is negative. As I conduct Aiki workshops around the country, people come to me with conflicts they are having in their lives. It may be a relationship they are in, the type of work they do, a health problem, or a general dissatisfaction with their life. They inevitably speak of the conflict as bad: "I don't want it. I have to do something about it. It's harmful."

Our first myth: Conflict Is Negative.

Nature doesn't see conflict as negative. Nature uses conflict as a primary motivator for change. Imagine floating down the Colorado River through the Grand Canyon. Quiet water flowing into exhilarating rapids. Hidden canyons with shade trees and wildflowers. Clear springs of drinkable water. Solitude and silence that can be found in few places in today's world. And those majestic cliffs looming above, with fantastic patterns in the rock and all the colors of the rainbow displayed. The Grand Canyon is truly one of the world's great wonders and provides us with a profound sense of harmony and peace. Yet how was that amazing vista formed? Eons and eons of water flowing, continually wearing away the rock, carrying it to the sea. A conflict that continues to this day. Conflict isn't negative, it just is.

In the Orient in the 1920s there lived a master of the martial arts, or the art of dealing with physical conflict. He was, by all standards of the time, a very successful man. Historically, a master had to be prepared to accept, and to meet victoriously, many challenges put forth by opponents interested in gaining fame or recognition. Often the loser was incapacitated or seriously injured as a result of these challenges, so there was obviously a high motivation to win.

This particular martial artist was consistently victorious. And yet even after reaching the pinnacle of success, he felt a deep and growing lack of fulfillment within. He took an extraordinary and unique step to discover this essential but missing ingredient by giving up the traditional way of the martial arts and going to the mountains, to return to nature and the land as a farmer and as a spiritual seeker.

---

In the spring of 1925, if I remember correctly, when I was taking a walk in the garden by myself, I felt that the universe suddenly quaked and that a golden spirit sprang up from the ground, veiled my body, and changed my body into a golden one.

At the same time my mind and body became light. I was able to understand the whispering of the birds, and was clearly aware of the mind of God, the Creator of this universe.

At that moment I was enlightened: the source of *budo* is God's love —the spirit of loving protection for all beings. Endless tears of joy streamed down my cheeks.[3]

After years of ascetic life and personal training, an entirely different state of consciousness permeated his being. He eventually came down from the mountains and astonished the martial artists in the land by declaring, "The true martial art is love." The physically oriented martial artists' typical reply was something along the lines of, "Thank you for sharing; now let's fight!" He found himself having to put his philosophy into practice. Challengers would inevitably find themselves upside down and immobilized in some unique manner, astonished that they were not hurt in the process. And he now met challengers effortlessly and joyfully, without the pain and strain of the past.

This remarkable Japanese martial artist, Morihei Ueshiba (1883-1969) had given birth to the art of aikido. It is now a highly sophisticated martial art. Its readily observable purpose is to resolve physical conflict by making an attack harmless without doing harm even to the attacker. However, as I have discovered over my many years of training in the art, far more useful is what it does to the practitioner. Aikido turns him upside down, shakes out all of those hard-earned patterns of struggling and stressing through life, and rips up all those acquired opinions about strength, power, relaxation, and relationships.

Oddly enough, I discovered aikido through resistance. I had been in love with the martial arts since I was about ten years old, when my Dad brought home my first set of boxing gloves. I would gather my friends from the neighborhood for weekend "world championships," with a serving spoon and a big metal bowl as my bell to begin the rounds, two bar stools for the corners, and the backyard fence enclosing the largest ring in the world. You could run but you couldn't hide. Bloody noses, crying, feigned death, and the bell were the only salvation for the sufficiently bludgeoned. Even though I added the arts of wrestling and karate to my boxing "studies" over the years, the joy of combat was most fulfilled in that all-American sport, football. From fifth grade through college, I was fed a diet of famous locker room philosophy: "When the going gets tough, the tough get going" and "No pain, no gain." Even as I hobbled away after my senior year in college with three missing front teeth and a history of broken bones, torn ligaments, and muscle pulls, I was still convinced I was on the right path. Of course, I had mistakenly equated toughness with rigidity, and pain with injury. If I had a difficulty, I could always handle it through lifting heavier weights, running more wind sprints, or clenching my teeth or fists. A breakthrough performance literally meant *breaking* through, whether it was wood or another human being. To make matters worse I got to be pretty good at it, which only reinforced my belief that more would be better.

When I first heard of the unique art called aikido, in which a small, physically weaker person could effortlessly throw or control a far larger and physically stronger person, I was obviously skeptical. I had been studying a variety of the "kicking and punching" arts when I first met an aikido expert, Rod Kobayashi. This 5'2" man of about forty years of age seemed to be having a great time, whirling and dancing around the mat as one man after another attacked him only to find themselves falling head over heels or completely immobilized by the lightest touch of his hands. All my years of fighting through life suddenly seemed to take on a gross and clumsy nature in comparison. More disconcerting was the fact that everyone seemed to be having so much fun. Even while falling, the attackers had such grace, fluidity, and joy that they also seemed to be winners, even though they were the ones careening from one side of the mat to the other.

I reassured my ego and justified my years of tough teeth-clenching with the thought that this must be a choreographed dance. It would never happen if I were the attacker. After all, I was just too strong and too tough. I watched as Mr. Kobayashi and a man a foot taller than he got down on their knees and began to do an energy development exercise. The larger man would grab the *sensei* (the Japanese word for "teacher") by the forearms and try to push him over. Smiling and laughing all the while, Mr. Kobayashi sent the bigger man rolling over on his back again and again.

*Now, wait just a minute,* I thought. *The dancelike stuff is one thing I can't really relate to or evaluate. But this activity looks like a simple case of physical strength, with each guy trying to push the other over. Why is the big guy faking it and rolling on his back?*

The *sensei* must have picked up on my perplexed look of disbelief. He smiled at me and asked me if I would like to join them. *Time to button up my chin strap,* I thought as I unconsciously took on my football/gladiator physiognomy and swaggered over to demonstrate my great physical prowess. As we kneeled face to face across from one another, I was outwardly very congenial. But inside, it was him or me, win/lose, dog eat dog all the way. After all, isn't that the way life is? He extended his arms to me. As I reached to grab them with a hard, tight, viselike grip, I was immediately disoriented. It was as if I had grabbed two active firehoses. There was no tension or rigidity. I had expected the feeling of grabbing a stiff piece of pipe. Instead there was, on the surface, a certain softness and pliability. Yet when I squeezed his arms, they felt as full and powerful as if rivers were flowing through them. As I began to tighten and puff up my muscles and power my way over him, a second shock hit me. I pushed and strained and grimaced to no avail. It felt as absurd as pushing a mountain. Embarrassed, I slacked up from my toil to see the *sensei* smiling happily at me. Nothing was going on. No sweat, no struggle, no strain. Then, although there was no change in his expression or show of force, I found myself falling over backward. My immediate thought was, *No way. I wasn't really trying. He took me by surprise.* Next time I grabbed tighter and pushed harder. More struggle, more strain.

Again I found myself on my back, staring up at the lights. But I was dazzled by another light, the one that had just been turned on inside my mind. During all those years, I had thought I knew what strength and power were all about, and here I was being thrown around like a child. I began to empty my full cup of knowledge. The contents were no longer appetizing in comparison to what I had just tasted. Could it be possible to live peacefully and happily *and* be strong? And all of this without the strain and the struggle?

The principles of aikido are applicable to much more than physical conflicts. As we will see, they can be applied to daily conflicts in business, education, and the arts. As we begin to embrace conflict as a prime motivator for change in our lives, we begin to see it as an opportunity. We are able to use it effectively for nurturing growth in ourselves and in our relationships.


*Nature goes her own way, and all that to us seems an exception is really according to order.*

                                                            Goethe

*Effective communication between the parties is
all but impossible if each plays to the gallery.*

Roger Fisher and William Ury
*Getting to Yes*

# 3. Conflict≠Contest

Equating conflict with contest is another myth we have been perpetuating for centuries.

Have you ever been upset when the boss differs with your suggestion, or the kids rebel at your ideas, or your spouse does just the opposite of what you expect? What is your knee-jerk reaction? Is it based on your fear of losing? The fear of being wrong? The need to prove yourself, to have your own way, to be right? When conflict becomes a win-lose contest in our minds, we immediately try to "win." The big question is, was there really a contest in the first place?

Ocean waves, powerful and majestic, incessantly break along coastlines throughout the world. What did it take to create this awesome splendor? *Conflict*—interference patterns between land, wind, and water. Who lost in this conflict? Was it the wind? Or the water? Obviously, neither lost.

Conflict is *not* contest. Conflict just *is*. We choose whether to make it a contest, a game in which there are winners and losers.

We are so patterned in our lives to think of conflict as contest that life becomes a big scoreboard. Every time a conflict arises, our minds see it light up in the heavens. Winning has become very important for most of us. Even those of us who aren't very competitive think of losing as something to avoid. Competitively oriented or not, we tend to treat life like a big tally sheet. Our need to win often takes precedence over resolving the conflict. It's as if we need 10,000 points to get to heaven. So, we have to work really hard to be right and to win. After all, wouldn't it be a catastrophe if we got to heaven's gate with only 9,999 points?

The part of us that wants to win and to be right every time inevitably does something inappropriate or foolish or worse. In our myopic efforts to make the world behave "perfectly," our antics can be the stuff of comedy, but more often are the cause of needless suffering.

Take our good friend, Joe Baggodonuts. Joe has worked hard all week. It's Saturday afternoon. He's watching the ball game, beer in hand, finally able to relax. Outside the front door is Betty Baggodonuts. Now, Betty has thirty pounds of groceries in each arm. She has a kid hanging on each leg. She has to open the door with her teeth. She staggers past Joe in the living room and barely makes it to the kitchen, groceries and kids attached, in an amazing juggling act which only a housewife of the magnitude of Betty Baggodonuts could perform. She gets everything together on the kitchen table, nobody gets injured—a miraculous feat has been accomplished.

As she stands at the table, she happens to glance back into the living room. She spots the unsuspecting Joe. Do you think that in her mind's eye she is seeing a sensitive, loving, and helpful husband? Not a chance, as before her sits the detestable, good-for-nothing blob who always leaves his socks on the floor. Sound familiar?

It doesn't take much time for her to react.

"Are you going to watch that stupid set all day long!"

Do you think old Joe's response is, "Ah, conflict. What a splendid opportunity!"?

Absolutely not. Instead, the "good-husband scoreboard" in the sky lights up. He gets sixty points if he can prove that he can be a good husband and still watch the ballgame. So the "tennis match" begins. He grabs his racket, grits his teeth, and gets right into the action.

Joe takes her serve with a sharply hit backhand, saying, "Yeah, well all you do is spend my money all day long." The issue has suddenly switched to money.

Wow! Great return! The ball shoots down the line.

Betty is no slouch. She moves over for the forehand and whacks it perfectly with "You never help out with the children." Quickly the issue has shifted again.

So he charges the net for that one: "I work my tail off and all you do is sit around and gossip with your girlfriends all day." Another issue to be reckoned with.

The contest is on. It's serve, backhand, forehand, go for the kill, search and destroy. It's a contest. Winning becomes the *only* thing.

But the conflict was never really about TV or money or children, was it? It could have been triggered by Betty's feelings of loneliness, her need for support and assurance, her need to communicate her frustrations, or just plain fatigue. Instead of expressing her true feelings and her needs, she jumps right into center court.

Joe, on the other hand, doesn't see the issue as "Clearly, somebody wants to communicate. Somewhere here is an opportunity for me. I'd like to discover what is really going on." All he sees are Betty's points flashing on the scoreboard, and he says to himself, "I can't lose this one." The battle begins. Expressing the real conflict and finding ways to support each other's needs doesn't happen when we're caught up in the "conflict as contest" mythology. We go for the win. We have to be right. The myth continues.

How do we break out of this old pattern and use conflict as an opportunity? How do we deal with the Joe and Betty Baggodonuts in each of us? I've picked a ludicrous name simply because the situation is so ludicrous. We beat ourselves up so mercilessly in contests we have created out of our imagined need to be right, when what we really need is to take ourselves more lightly, which will enable us to move more easily to an appropriate resolution of the conflict.

A

# AIKIDO

The martial art of aikido (as pictured in photograph A) offers a useful metaphor for shifting our way of thinking and acting in conflict situations. Using aikido, we are able to experience the resolution of physical conflicts, actual bodily attacks, without the use of unnecessary force. Attacks are neutralized without injury. Life is protected and nurtured. When we experience this unique approach working effectively on a physical level, we are much more able to let go of solidified beliefs and inappropriate patterns of reaction in the rest of our lives.

In photograph B, my assistant, Tom Eckstein (left), is demonstrating a grabbing type of attack. I react in the typical mode of perceiving conflict as contest. My reaction is the traditional one of grabbing back and getting caught up in a fight. As my mind freezes on the grab and I occupy myself in trying to break loose from the attacker's grasp, I play right into his game—fighting. A person attacking you on a physical level has usually sized up the situation and chooses to attack because he thinks he has an advantage. (This reveals one of my favorite secrets of the martial arts—that you are rarely attacked by midgets.)

B                                    C

Aikido, literally translated, means "the way of blending energy."
In this light, all of life, including a physical attack, is energy with which
to dance. Attacks are considered just another of the endless gifts of
energy to be used creatively and harmoniously. Given this shift of
perspective, notice my response in photograph C. I'm using a very
important principle in aikido, the ability to honor and acknowledge
the energy given, instead of opposing it. Notice the attacker's balance as I move out of the way and align *with* the direction and the
intensity of his attack. His weakened position dissipates the power of
his attack and allows him to be led easily, so that the injurious nature
of the attack is neutralized.

A second important element of aikido, evident in photograph C,
is the principle of acceptance. I am accepting his grab and literally
embracing it, rather than trying to get rid of it. I place my hand right
on top of his, making it a part of *me*, so that I can focus my attention
on what is more important than the issue of the hand on my shoulder
—the attacker himself. Whatever may follow, I am in a position to
direct the flow of energy instead of being pushed around by it.

The magic of aikido is that the blending does not stop here but continues until peace is established. In the photograph sequence on page 43, we see this principle in action. If the attacker comes with great forward momentum, I simply get out of the way and add my own energy to his. By getting out of the way, I remove the object of the attack. Expecting, but not getting, a rigid target, the assailant pitches forward, off balance, like a waiter with a full tray of entrees falling through a door that is unexpectedly opened from the other side. Sensitivity to the attacker's energy and the timing of one's response accordingly are essential to the art of aikido.

The attacker may not always do the expected and may indeed change the form of the attack at any time. Choosing to dance with the energy of the attacker allows one to be flexible enough to respond to the new form. The ability to dance keeps one from getting stuck on a particular strategy for resolution.

For example, in the sequence on pages 44–45, the attacker grabs and then pulls me toward him. By going with that new direction of energy, I am best able to avoid a struggle and to redirect the energy to a peaceful outcome. In the art of aikido, the blending movement puts one in an optimum position to apply one of the many immobilization techniques for neutralizing the harmful quality of an attack.

Let's use these principles from aikido to transform Joe and Betty Baggodonuts' emotional "tennis match" into a dance. What if instead of continuing to pile years of resentment on top of misunderstanding, Joe and Betty committed themselves to bringing life back into their relationship and to learning to flow with each other's energy?

First, let's examine the principle of acknowledgment. Instead of getting caught up in Betty's anger and immediately blitzing her front line like an NFL linebacker, what if Joe saw Betty's anger as pent-up stress needing to be released, and not necessarily an attack on himself? By simply recognizing it as useful incoming energy, Joe could have avoided his own urge toward hostility and, calmly acknowledging her upset, proceeded to give her the time and space to fully express her feelings.

For example, he could reply, "I've been so wrapped up in this game. I'm sorry I didn't notice you come in. Is there anything I can do to help you?"

I understand the difficulty in saying something like this in a relationship containing real tension and hostility. It takes a firm conviction that you have the ability to create powerful, mutually supportive relationships and a willingness to do what is necessary to make that vision a reality. Sincerely acknowledging someone even in the heat of anger or irritation takes knowing what you really want in a relationship. (By acknowledging Betty's upset, Joe opens himself to receiving her energy, thereby showing that he values their relationship.)

Obviously, Joe's reply may not be in the exact words that you would use. It is not the precise language that is important here. It is the quality of sincerity and the intention that convey the real message. The fact that Joe made an effort makes the difference. If Betty's real need is simply to be acknowledged, then Joe's new statement has done much to end the conflict right there. (Her upset having been released and not resisted, she is able to communicate a real desire in a way that also acknowledges Joe. )

"After the game, will you play with the kids so I can have some time to myself?"

As I'm sure you have experienced, it isn't always this easy. For instance, Betty may be so upset at that moment that she's unable to appreciate or even hear Joe's sincerity. She launches another assault:

"For starters, you can turn off that stupid game and spend some time with *your* children."

Joe may respond in many different and appropriate ways. Regardless of what language he chooses, he needs to be clear in his acknowledgment of Betty's emotional state.

"I can hear that you are really upset," or "It sounds like you could really use a hand." In his commitment and desire to strengthen his relationship, Joe can also exclaim, "I'll be right there."

I can hear the reader saying at this point, "No way am I going to give in that easily," or "What if it's the fourth quarter with the game tied?" Remember, what we are talking about here comes from a commitment to transforming a relationship from contest and win/lose to something far more powerful. You can rest assured that there will be times when Joe must consciously change his traditional patterned reaction.

Of course, if there is a critical moment in the game, he can state the truth cheerfully (and the important word here is _cheerfully_), "I'll be there in a couple of minutes."

Joe proceeds to turn off the TV and show up in the kitchen. Such an immediate willingness to respond despite the derogatory nature of Betty's attack requires calmness and the ability to let go of the ego's need to fight back and be right. If done with a sincere desire to resolve the conflict, the communication will not be that of a whipped puppy dog reluctantly coming forward with his tail between his legs. In fact, it most often will be received by Betty as a real gift of strength, appreciation, and support. The response to a gift such as this is usually a gift in return.

"Thanks, Joe. I really don't want you to miss all of the game. Maybe you could take the kids afterward or even do something with them while you watch the game."

Of course, if Betty continues the attack, at least Joe will know that the real issue is not appreciation, television, or the kids. Just by being there and aligning himself with her energy, he finds himself in a far more powerful position to discover the real issue and to get on with this opportunity to resolve it.

Joe or Betty can win the battle of the TV at the risk of damaging their relationship, or they can take care of the vital issues of relationship now and have true peace when the Super Bowl comes around. If their relationship is truly sound, it will weather those occasions when Joe is locked into a three-point stance in front of the TV while his socks are strewn around him like so many wide receivers.

When one is willing to see all conflicts—whether physical, emotional, or mental—as dances of energy, and to accept them and to blend with them, options and opportunities for successful resolution emerge, powerfully and elegantly. The ability to remove the unfortunate contest-mentality from conflict takes courage, tact, a sense of well-being, and a strong commitment to developing fulfilling relationships. Booker T. Washington, the great black educator who founded Tuskegee Institute in Alabama in the 1880s, was once walking past the mansion of a very wealthy plantation owner. The white mistress of the household, not knowing him by sight, yelled out at him to chop some firewood. Professor Washington calmly threw off his coat, seized the nearby axe, cut a pile of wood, and proceeded to carry it to the kitchen as requested. He smiled pleasantly at the plantation owner and went on his way. After he had gone, one of the servant girls told the mistress, "That was Professor Washington."

The following day, the embarrassed mistress went to Washington's office to apologize.

"It's entirely all right, Madam," Washington responded. "I like to work and I'm delighted to do favors for my friends." In that moment, Professor Washington created a true friend, who supported him by raising thousands of dollars for the institute.

The ability to respond to our own conflicts in such an effective manner is an art. The Aiki Approach will provide you with a deeper understanding of the principles and skills necessary to become such an artist—to prosper from and even enjoy those minor and major struggles that we face each day.

The Aiki Approach is a method for resolving conflict that combines my study and teaching in the martial arts with my work in business and education. Throughout the book, the word *Aiki* will refer to the blending or harmonizing aspect of daily life and to the skills necessary to resolve conflict. The word *aikido* will be used to refer to the specific martial art. As we recognize that all conflict gives us an opportunity to dance rather than struggle, our movements and actions take on a spirit of joy and harmony that permeates all concerned. In the following chapters, we will examine more closely the principles of the Aiki Approach—the principles of centering, relaxing, awareness, and flexibility—and how we can use them at home, at school, or in the office.

*Would you rather be right or happy?*
        Jerry Jampolsky

# THE NATURE OF CONFLICT

*Conflict is natural; neither positive nor negative, it just is.*

Conflict is just an interference pattern of energies.

Nature uses conflict as its primary motivator for change, creating beautiful beaches, canyons, mountains, and pearls.

It's not whether you have conflict in your life. It's what you do with that conflict that makes a difference.

*Conflict is not a Contest.*

Winning and losing are goals for games, not for conflicts.

Learning, growing, and cooperating are goals for resolving conflicts.

Conflict can be seen as a gift of energy, in which neither side loses and a new dance is created.

Resolving conflict is rarely about who is right. It *is* about acknowledgment and appreciation of differences.

Conflict begins within. As we unhitch the burden of belief systems and heighten our perceptions, we love more fully and freely.

# THE AIKI
# APPROACH

# 4. Choose to Be Centered

We sit around in a ring and suppose
But the Secret sits in the middle and knows.
*Robert Frost*

The Aiki Approach presents conditions that each of us can *choose* to create at *any* time. It allows us to break through to a state of artistry, a state beyond success. It allows for conflicts in our lives to be resolved naturally and peacefully, with all sides being mutually supported, and it brings us closer in touch with our true self: a fully integrated mind, body, and spirit.

The first condition of the Aiki Approach is:

1. CHOOSE TO BE CENTERED.

Notice that it doesn't say *try* or *hope*. Talking about being calm or balanced is one thing. *Being* it is something else. The above condition says *choose*. Centering is a real psychophysiological experience that each of us can choose to have, right now.

We have all experienced centering. It occurs when the mind, body, and spirit become fully integrated in dynamic balance and connectedness with the world around us. There is a heightened awareness and sensitivity, a feeling that everything is perfect the way it is. The truth of who we are as human beings is revealed.

This quality of centeredness is always there during those magic moments of your life. Those could be taking your first successful steps as a young child, being tucked in at night by Mom or Dad, making the big play in sports, conquering your fear of speaking in front of people, sitting quietly by a river, or just being with someone you love.

World champion downhill skier Franz Klammer had that quality when he "miraculously" recovered time after time from near disaster in his wild fling down an icy mountain in his homeland of Austria to capture the 1976 Olympic gold medal. Martin Luther King was the embodiment of centeredness as he led thousands of civil rights activists down the streets of Birmingham, Alabama, on Good Friday of 1963, knowing he was on his way to jail. And as he looks into the loving eyes of his mother while breast feeding, an infant tells us that he, too, is centered.

The centered state is simple, natural, and powerful. Understanding center is useful only if we truly integrate it into our mind and body and use it. More often, however, we intellectualize and philosophize about centering, rarely using it or making it an integral part of our being and our daily life.

Physicists have defined the center of gravity of an object as an infinitely small point upon which the entire object can be balanced. You can take the local grocery store or the car you drive or your own body and balance it on that one infinitely small point. This is not just an intellectual concept, nor is it merely a physical location that can be marked with a magic marker. It is a dynamically active, vibrationally alive center of balance and stability. By understanding and cultivating the skill of centering, you will dramatically affect your ability to live an active and vital life. Those rare magic moments can become your daily routine. Does it seem outrageous that all this is possible simply by your becoming centered? Maybe so, but it works!

## CAPTURING THE CENTERED STATE

Centering is something we can understand and *choose* to experience. The first step in integrating centeredness into your life is to experience your own center on a psychophysiological level. Through a simple exercise, we can validate and verify the effect that centering has on our physical and emotional stability. Following these directions, you can help a partner experience the centered state.

- Have a partner stand easily and naturally, with his feet approximately shoulder width apart.
- Stand beside him, facing in the same direction, so that he feels you are there to support him, not compete with him.
- Reach over and place the fingertips of one hand very lightly just above the center of your partner's chest.
- Very slowly and smoothly increase the pressure on that point, as if you were going to push him directly back. Do so smoothly, with no jerky or sudden motion. Have your partner stand naturally and not try to physically resist this pressure.
- Your partner soon will begin to wobble. Notice how little pressure it took for this to occur.
- Keeping your fingertips in the same position on his chest, ask your partner to concentrate on his center—the physical center of his body—which, in a standing position, is located roughly a couple of inches below the navel. Having him touch that area with his finger will help him to focus his mind on the location.
- Slowly increase the pressure again, gently so as not to distract his thoughts away from his center. It may be helpful to tell him to take any feeling of pressure on the chest down to his center, to actually feel it "from his center."
- As you slowly increase the pressure on his chest you will find that there is remarkably more stability, gained simply by your partner's becoming more aware of his natural center.

In contrast, place a finger of your free hand on the tip of his nose. Have him concentrate his mind there (it won't take long—it's such a *ludicrous* feeling) and test as before. There's the wobble again. Then repeat the test with his attention back on his center. Stability! Have your partner concentrate on various other parts of the body, such as the top of his foot (you can touch it with your foot to help focus his attention) or the top of his head, and test. Again, instability will be evident. Always allow your partner time to put his mind as completely as possible on the chosen location before applying pressure. And keep all other variables (your partner's body position and muscle tension, the location of your fingers, etc.) the same, so that you have a more accurate measure of the difference that centering plays in your partner's basic stability. Between tests on different areas of the body, always come back to the center test, allowing your partner to recapture the centered feeling. Always complete the exercise with the centered feeling so that it is imprinted deeply in the conscious and subconscious. You can further support this process by acknowledging your partner verbally with an enthusiastic "yes" or "excellent" when you feel that he is centered. When finished, reverse roles with your partner and repeat the exercise.

The purpose of this exercise is to capture the quality of centering in an experiential way. When I work with people individually, or in an Aiki workshop setting, we don't just talk about it. We do it. We take the time to experience, taste, touch, and feel the power of centeredness. This is where true change occurs.

For one person, the centered state will be internally experienced as a feeling, for another as a vibration, and for another as a vision. It could be a combination of these. The important thing is that you imprint the experience deeply in your own way and can make clear distinctions between the centered and the uncentered state.

Another remarkable demonstration is to face your partner, place your hands under his arms, and lift him straight up. It would be advisable here to use a partner of comparable size and strength. Have him concentrate on the top of his head. Bend your knees and, lifting primarily with your legs, lift him straight up. Notice the amount of strength it takes you to do so. Mentally register the approximate amount of weight that you are lifting. Try not to pull your partner forward and off balance, as it will negate the controlled nature of the experiment. (After all, one can't be centered *and* off balance.) Next have him think centered and try to lift again. If his mind stays concentrated at the center point, it will feel like he has suddenly swallowed an entire set of barbells. Centeredness adds not only stability, but substance.

# DAILY PRACTICE

*Nothing less than becoming one with the universe will suffice.*
                                            Morihei Ueshiba

Centeredness is a true psychophysiological phenomenon that affects everything in your environment. It may appear difficult to comprehend on an intellectual level. It is only through experiencing centering that it can become comprehensible *and* useful.

Have you ever heard the term "mind and body integration"? Well, here it is in a simple yet extremely effective form. The mind and body are intimately connected, and it is easy to begin to experience this profoundly through these simple exercises. It is recapturing that experience throughout the day that allows you to repattern your mind and body into greater unification and stability.

This does not mean that you walk around *thinking* one point or center throughout the day. Not only would that appear foolish, it would prove ineffective as you ran into walls and people and forgot what you were supposed to be doing. Instead, periodically throughout the day, take a few seconds to recapture or reexperience the centered feeling that you acquired during the centering exercise and then go about your normal routine. Great athletes, artists, and professionals in all fields are not *trying* to be centered when they are performing at an optimum level—they are fully committed and concentrated on the job at hand. They are *operating* from centeredness, not thinking about it. Through years of practice, the "greats" have acquired, unconsciously, a certain quality of centeredness. We can optimize our own progress toward excellence by understanding and using centering *now*.

Practice and repetition bring results. There are many opportunities to practice in our daily lives. Those uncomfortable moments when conflict arises are perfect places to test the power of this centered state. You'll find that it is impossible to be angry, fearful, or at the mercy of the conflict in any emotional or physical way and still be centered.

Remember the old adage that you should "count to ten" before reacting in a conflict situation? The opportunity is yours to make this old adage really work. When that feeling of upset or irritation comes, or when fear begins to build, see and hear a big *Yes!* flash in technicolor and quadraphonic sound in your mind, then a big *Thank you for this opportunity.*

Take a moment to become centered. Take a deep breath, and on exhaling, fully release the energy you are feeling, all the while returning to center. This can be done quietly, in a nondisturbing manner. This moment of centering will give you time to really receive the communication, to silently acknowledge the situation. You can always excuse yourself and go into another room if you feel the release is more appropriately done in privacy. The main thing is to breathe deeply and return to that integrated state, to your deepest level of clarity and personal power—which also connects you sensitively and responsibly to the environment around you. You will begin to realize that it's OK to feel upset and fearful because now you don't have to operate out of those states. The energy can be released in positive and appropriate ways. Each time you recapture that centered feeling, you will find the anger or emotion naturally diminishes and your response to the conflict is appropriate and harmonious.

In the beginning stages of centering, there will be a tendency to react with the old patterns of fear or anger before remembering to respond from your center. In time, you will be able to make more subtle distinctions between the two and expand your centeredness into larger areas of your life—many of which you may have considered beyond your control. No longer can you pretend to be a victim. Your life becomes a conscious choice. It's hard not to smile when you're truly centered.

## SOME HEAVY THOUGHTS

Aikido has a way of derailing us from the straight and narrow track of our accustomed ways and exposing the closed-minded part of ourselves. In doing seminars throughout the country, I occasionally find myself at the conferences of special groups such as business people, educators, law enforcement agencies, or medical doctors. I am a scheduled presenter among others who have discussed subjects that are comfortable and directly related to the conferees' professions. There has been no advance publicity as to the unusual nature of my presentation or on the art of aikido. When I first appear on stage wearing the garb of an aikido instructor—black flowing skirt (*hakama*), white "karate" *gi* top—with wooden staff and swords in hand, I wonder whether I have been suddenly transported to a strange and alien planet. I can feel the closed-minded shutting their mental doors and hear the nervous sound of latching and bolting as they scurry to protect their prized (and sometimes unexamined) belief systems.

"What does this 'karate stuff' have to do with being a doctor?" Or "Oh boy, I can turn my mind off now and sit back and enjoy the entertainment. Maybe he'll break some bricks with his head. . . ."

Instead of resorting to marginally effective intellectual arguments on the appropriateness and applicability of aikido and the Aiki Approach to their profession, I simply recapture my centered feeling, begin a demonstration, and immediately the calm, good feelings of rapport begin to emerge. Within minutes spectators become participants, experiencing rather than debating the power and grace of aikido. They witness strikes, kicks, and grabs being neutralized and controlled in a whirling, dancelike joyful manner, with no harm being done to the attacker. I can sense their minds opening and their interest building.

I begin to explore with them the power of centering. I ask for the two biggest, strongest people I can find in the audience. I stand between the two in a normal stance and ask them to grab my forearms with both hands, bend down into a squat position, and lift me off the ground. Since I only weigh 150 pounds, they lift me quickly and easily, two or three feet off the ground. Upon returning to earth, I explain that I am now going to get centered. At first glance it appears that nothing has changed. I'm standing and looking the same way, and they attempt to lift me in the same manner. But this time nothing moves. They can't lift me. As the audience watches the straining, struggling, and grunting of the two lifters, I can hear the mental computers throughout the room blowing fuses, and rigid mind-sets sparking and short-circuiting all around me. These intelligent people recognize that I didn't suddenly gain 2500 pounds. And yet some remarkable change occurred.

I then become uncentered by focusing my mind elsewhere, such as on the top of my head, and have the two men lift again. I ask them to hold me suspended in the air. They do so easily. While they are supporting me, I explain that we often find ourselves anxious, uncentered, "failing," when we are going for it, really stretching ourselves and taking risks in life. But at any time we can *choose* to be centered. At this point, I do exactly that and immediately find myself back on the ground, with two stunned and straining men baffled by the sudden change and their inability to keep me up in the air. It is as if an elevator had just broken loose. The remaining latches and bolts of the rigid minds in the audience fly open, and I can feel the audience become like children, naturally open to exploring new concepts playfully rather than simply debating them intellectually. When I explain that this and other exercises are available to all of them right now, that they are simple and natural and not limited to a special few, the vision of their own potential expands. They become open to the true explanation of why the exercise works.

The exercise works because centering has a positive effect not so much on physical weight as on your *relationship* to the world around you and consequently on how others relate to you. When a person chooses that centered state, the environment around him literally feels the positive influence. That hushed, electrical feeling that flows through a crowd, that air of confidence that radiates when a John F. Kennedy walks to a podium, a Jack Nicklaus strolls onto a putting green, or a Frank Sinatra saunters toward a microphone is a quality that is available to all of us. We are not discussing mere philosophical concepts, but the reality of living more powerfully in our daily lives.

## CAN LIFE BE A PLAYGROUND?

We have all experienced moments when we felt good about ourselves and recognized our relationship to something bigger and more powerful than our immediate surroundings or occupation. Centering allows us to see the world from a larger perspective. We do not become a victim of every conflict or get trapped into a patterned negative reaction.

Imagine yourself taking time out from your busy schedule to wander freely and enjoy the day. You notice a playground. You wander over and find yourself in a sandbox with a group of small children, just playing, experiencing the joys of childhood, building sandcastles. A little three-year-old, for some reason, kicks over her castle, then walks over and kicks over yours. Do you notice that you don't pick her up by the hair and sling her across the playground, bucket and all? Instead you are naturally more loving and understanding with her. Your life is not dependent on this little sandbox and what happens to your little castle. You have a prior place of fulfillment and relationship much larger than the playground. You recognize the playground for what it is, a place to experience, to enjoy, and to make mistakes.

What would it be like if we dealt with the world around us as a playground, full of children learning and growing? Would this perspective allow us to deal with others in a more compassionate and loving way?

Being centered in conflict provides us with a sense of spaciousness and nonattachment. As we expand our mental sandboxes through centering, our awareness and sensitivity to the environment around us increases. We move beyond our personal struggles and concerns into a larger perspective. When a conflict arises, such as a sudden injury, a heated dispute with an angry colleague or spouse, or even a great loss or setback, miraculously we find ourselves operating calmly, compassionately, and appropriately.

When Anne Sullivan arrived in Alabama to work with an "impossible" case, an insolent and wild, blind deaf-mute named Helen Keller, the attitude of the distraught family was "What are we going to do *with* her" rather than "What can we do *for* her." Anne Sullivan had experienced circumstances as bad as Helen's in her own life. Her drunken father beat her. She had been starved, battered, neglected, and finally abandoned. She had been blind herself, her eyesight restored through surgery. Her centered state did not waver when she stepped from her carriage and first met Helen. Her clarity of perspective was such that she saw far beyond a difficult and incurable little girl. She saw a human being feeling trapped in solitary confinement and willing to do anything to break through her sense of isolation. Anne Sullivan knew that the pent-up energy of pain and anger could become the unlimited drive for learning and excellence if only a small window of possibility could be opened. After she removed Helen from her normal home environment, there began a fierce battle of wills that raged for days. From a state of centeredness, Anne Sullivan weathered the storm with love. Literally spending hours on end physically restraining Helen from destroying their cottage, she calmly held fast to her vision of what was possible.

"Her restless spirit gropes in the dark," Sullivan commented. "Her untaught, unsatisfied hands destroy whatever they touch because they do not know what else to do with things."[4]

Anne Sullivan did not fall victim to rage or pity. Within a couple of weeks, the window of light opened. While she poured cold water over Helen's right hand and spelled w-a-t-e-r with her finger in Helen's left hand, Helen became transfixed, truly centered—the universe within her became united with the universe without. A new linkage of clear communication riveted her. Life had shifted from a prison to a playground.

## LIGHT OR LAMPSHADE?

When you are centered, you become more powerfully you. You become authentic. So much of our lives is spent off center—doing what we think we *should* do to get everyone's approval. "I should do this, I should do that," we tell ourselves, hoping someone will notice what we're doing, while deep inside we feel like we're being "should on."

It becomes an internal source of conflict. We may be aware on some level that we are the light, but we go on decorating, adjusting and changing the lampshade, the ego, so it will look just right to others. By centering, we naturally return to being the light—lighting up and radiating out.

I had a valuable lesson in centeredness and authenticity in Japan. I had an opportunity to visit Mount Koya-san, one of the largest and oldest Buddhist monasteries. Its history goes back hundreds of years

—it was founded in 816 A.D. by Kobo Daishi. At one time there were fifty thousand monks in residence. Being there was like being thrust back into ancient Japan—I was surrounded by traditional clothing; Zen gardens and ponds; uncluttered, simple, and immaculately kept rooms. I was awestruck by the history, spirituality, and serenity.

I had the opportunity to have an interview with the abbot, the spiritual leader of the monastery. He had just returned from a six-month retreat. The thought kept recurring, *How does one "retreat" from a monastery?* Take up residence in an isolation tank? Bury one-self in the desert? Live naked in a tree?

Throughout the night I meditated and wondered what the abbot would do with me. I was transported in mind and body to about 1600 A.D., the heart of the Tokugawa shogunate, fully dressed in samurai garb and calmly waiting to discover the essence of Self. Would the abbot give me one of those intricate *koans* (Zen puzzles) that would catapult me into "True Meaning"? Would he slap me on the back with the *shinai* (bamboo staff) and knock the "Great Sense" into me? Would there be a touch of *darshon* (enlightenment)? Images of mind-shattering *koans*, simple bowls of rice, rigorous martial art training, and waterfall meditations floated through my mind during the day and into the night. I was like a child on Christmas Eve.

Finally, the next morning came, and a little monk knocked and opened my *shoji* screen. "Master is ready to see you now."

I tightened the belt on my kimono, leaped into my sandals, and scurried down the wooden plankway around the Zen gardens and ponds to the interview room. It was an exquisitely crafted room, with a beautiful flower-covered altar. And there he was, sitting comfort-ably, rather than stoically, in a *zazen* (cross-legged) position, a che-rubic old man in his eighties. He had an ageless demeanor, twinkling eyes, a joyful sense all about him. He was just as I had pictured him.

Upon entering, I sat directly across the room from him, basking in his serenity. After a very peaceful while, he asked me in broken En-glish whether I would like to ask him anything.

Now, I had been thinking all night about what to ask him that would really give me that magic, that stroke of enlightenment. So all pumped up and ready, I said, "*Sensei,* what was the most enlighten-ing moment of your life, the one that really shifted you into another state of consciousness?"

*Ah, what a great question,* I thought as I sat back. *Here it comes. Magic from the master about to arrive.*

He closed his eyes, opened them slowly, and with a twinkle in them said, "Los Angeles, 1932, Boy Scouts."

My stoic, meditative position crumbled; my chin collapsed into my kimono. *You have to be kidding,* I thought. I'd come halfway around the world to discover ancient truths hidden deep in the Orient, climbed this mountain to meet the master, and he tells me "Boy Scouts in Los Angeles"? So much for my expectation of enlightenment.

He continued as if nothing were wrong, unbothered by my reaction.

"Oh yes, I was asked by my teacher to go to Los Angeles to set up a temple. And while I was doing that, one of my students there had a Boy Scout troop and asked me to help them. So I did, and oh, they were so wonderful, so loyal, so dedicated. I'd like my monks to be like that."

And then I got it—the whack upside my head. There he was, not doing something out of a desire for approval, not giving me what he thought I wanted. Instead of giving me the "proper lampshade" of my expectations, he gave me his light. He came from center, from authenticity. This vibrant, happy old man was just being himself. He was not there to fulfill my "model" of how he should be. Instead he gave me a far greater gift—the quality of his being brought forth by his courage simply to be himself. My bells were rung. The "teaching" was complete.

When you are centered, you become more in touch with who you really are. The need for outside approval falls away. Your personal vision becomes clear. And this clarity is the point of power. It was out of this quality of centeredness that John F. Kennedy publicly took full responsibility for the ill-fated attack on Cuba, the Bay of Pigs fiasco in April of 1961.

When one is authentic, the trappings of success are unimportant. Will Rogers had all the money he would ever need from his newspaper columns and stage, radio, and movie appearances. Celebrity status, the kiss of death for so many, never derailed him from being himself. He basically wore the same style of clothing he had always worn, rumpled general-store suits and shirts. At the height of his success, his dressing room furnishings consisted of two old straight-backed wooden chairs. His wife, Betty, decided to surprise him by purchasing two soft, comfortable armchairs; a chaise lounge; drapes; lamps; an Oriental rug—everything a man of his stature deserved. Some days later, she walked into the dressing room expecting to find him relaxing on the chaise lounge. Instead, she found him sitting cross-legged on the floor. He couldn't find anyplace else that suited him. Even though he had sincerely thanked her for her thoughtfulness, Betty got the message. Back came the chairs. Like Will Rogers, they were simple and functional. Will Rogers was truly authentic. In that simple truth was his power and his influence. As he stated, "I use only one set method in my little gags and that is to try and keep to the truth."[5]

Sometimes the world pulls you in a direction which, in your heart, you do not wish to go. When you take the time to center yourself daily, you retouch the place of clarity within. You begin breathing deeply and fully from the source of your being and tapping the power necessary to live your life out of integrity. It's often uncomfortable if you feel dependent on approval from others. Whatever the discomfort, it is an acceptable price to pay for true freedom.

Heavyweight boxing champion Muhammad Ali was a man who had the world at his fingertips in 1966. A former Olympic champion and the current world champion, he was exactly where he wanted to be. Of course, the public had often disapproved of the outrageous behavior which resulted from his willingness to let his unique personality shine. However, the real test of his integrity came in 1966 when he was reclassified 1A and received his draft notice to join the Army and prepare for possible fighting in Vietnam. He took a stand which flew directly in the face of what was then strong public sentiment in support of the war. In following his sense of integrity, he accepted the risk of going to jail, the possible end of his career, and public shame.

---

I don't want to go to jail, but I've got to live the life my conscience and my God tells me to. What does it profit me to be the wellest-liked man in America who sold out to everybody.[6]

---

On April 28, 1967, in Houston, Texas, it wasn't the wild-eyed and zealous prefight Ali that people at the Army induction ceremonies observed. It was a centered, absolutely still man of conviction who quietly refused to step forward when his name was called.

That and his simple statement, "I ain't got nothing against them Viet Cong," began a public and government reaction that exiled him from his boxing career for three and a half years. Whatever one may think of what he chose to do, the fact is that he was willing to operate from his center and to abide by his deep personal values and beliefs. A little-known fact is that years earlier, during the Olympics, he had also had the courage of his convictions in telling the Soviet press, when they were pressing him about racial discrimination, "To me, the USA is still the best country in the world, including yours."[7] The man was simply courageous enough to be himself.

# THE GIFT OF MEDITATION

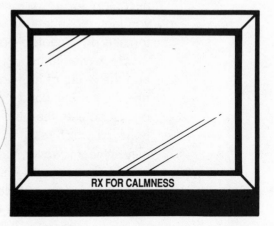

RX FOR CALMNESS

*All man's miseries derive from not being able to sit quietly in a room alone.*
Pascal

Consciousness can be viewed as a movie screen upon which the images and experiences of life appear. A distorted or wrinkled or cluttered screen creates a distorted, cluttered view. Cleaning the screen of our consciousness daily allows us to see the world freshly and clearly.

A book about centering wouldn't be complete if it failed to ad-

# A CENTERING EXERCISE

- Sit in a *comfortable* position in which your back can be held straight without straining.
- Close your eyes and take some long, deep breaths through your nostrils. With each long, slow exhalation, imagine you see the tension flowing out of your body from head to toe. Do this for a few minutes until you feel relaxed and comfortable.
- Let your breathing settle down naturally to its own pace.
- Imagine that you have a beam of light extending from your center through the top of your head. Picture your center as being about the size of a basketball.
- Let the light beam emanating from your center swing from side to side, taking your head and upper body with it as one unit. Let your swaying be easy and relaxed.
- After swaying back and forth for ten to fifteen seconds to establish a natural rhythm, let the swing and your center become half as large as before. Continue swaying with the same rhythm, but decrease the swing proportionately to the size of your "new" center.
- Continue in this process, every few seconds decreasing the size of the swing and of your center by half.
- Soon your body will cease to move physically and it may be difficult to picture the actual size of your center. Simply focus your attention on the vibration of your center diminishing in size to infinity. It is the vibratory quality of the swinging "pendulum of light" following a single, infinitely decreasing point that becomes the focus of your attention. It allows for a comfortable ride inward to the source of your being.
- When extraneous thoughts come into the mind, do not fight or struggle against them. Instead, easily come back to that vibratory quality of the center becoming smaller by half . . . half . . . half . . . and half again, on to infinity. The vibratory quality may be perceived differently by each individual and may change within an individual periodically throughout the exercise. It may be perceived as a feeling, a sound, or an image. Allow it to take whatever form it chooses.
- Continue this process for fifteen to twenty minutes. When ending the exercise, bring your awareness back to the breath and breathe deeply into each and every area of the body. Take a few moments to do this, as it allows you to come out of the process easily and brings your awareness back into your body and the immediate surroundings.

dress the subject of meditation. For me, my daily meditations are essential in quieting my mind and clearing the screen of my consciousness. Meditation has been a very special force in my life. But how can I discuss in a book a subject of such dimension, let alone teach such an art through the written word, when, after many years of meditation practice, I consider myself a mere novice? I would like, however, to share with you some of my thoughts, with the hope that you will consider exploring the techniques available to you. Meditation has been a precious gift to me, and I'd like to share some of what I do know about it.

Meditation is one of the most powerful tools available for integrating mind, body, and spirit—for centering on all levels of being. It has been practiced since the beginnings of civilization, and methods for quieting the mind are found in every culture, from the Judeo-Christian traditions to those of the Orient.

The spectrum of the meditation experience has no boundaries. The feelings range from the blissful to the powerful, the visions from all-encompassing light to unfathomable darkness, and the sounds from endless chatter to a single note. Regardless of the subjective experience, which may change each time you meditate, the gift you will be receiving will be a deeper understanding of who you are and an increased connection to the universe. And through regular practice, your increased sense of centeredness will be a gift to others.

Meditation is a very natural process. It may be for this reason that many of us find meditation so difficult. You see, we are quite accomplished at straining and struggling to receive the worthwhile things in life. So we grit our teeth and *try* to meditate. We forget how simple it can be.

Meditation is a surrendering technique—a technique of letting go, of trust and inner release. It is a technique in which you let go of that endless dialogue that goes on all day between your ears—that loquacious program that starts as soon as you open your eyes each morning. The commentary or soap opera is so continual that we often think it's the only channel on the air. Meditation is a way to get underneath this superficial thinking and come down to the source of thought—to that level of being that is naturally more powerful and which opens the doors to new levels of experience and action.

There are many meditation techniques available today. Yet despite all the differences, you will find that there is a commonality among them. They all use a simple "vehicle" that allows you a comfortable ride inward. We get so focused on the external aspects of ourselves that we rarely turn inward. When I ask people who they are, they will usually describe what kind of job they do, the relationships they have, their material possessions, their thoughts and belief systems. Meditation techniques are there to guide us effortlessly in a new direction—deep into the wellspring of our being.

The techniques of meditation vary mostly in their choice of a vehicle or thought to guide you inward. Tibetan techniques often focus on the breath or the heartbeat, an autonomic response. The Zen approach is one of witnessing or passive sitting. The vehicle used here is just to be aware, to experience whatever comes forth in the mind. The techniques from India frequently use mantras as vehicles. Transcendental meditation is a classic form of that technique. Mantras are vibratory sounds from the Sanskrit language. In Sanskrit, the oldest language known to man, the words or sounds themselves are derived from the vibratory quality that any object or form emits. Sound or energy wave patterns actually precede form. These sounds have a tremendous amount of power. The mantras are said to represent various aspects of God.

Christianity and Judaism are also steeped in meditation, though in their contemporary forms the ancient practice of meditation has been displaced in favor of outward action. One of the earliest Christian texts in English, *The Cloud of Unknowing,* thought to have been written by a priest in England in the second half of the fourteenth century, is essentially a textbook on meditation. The vehicle used is a simple thought or quality of the Christ or of God. It arises naturally from within during meditation. For Christians, meditation can be considered the listening aspect of prayer.

Action can also be meditative. The whirling dervishes of the mystical Islamic cults are engaged in a very sophisticated form of mind/ body concentration. The intense, repeated, focused movement brings their consciousness to a very high level. Most of the meditation techniques available from around the world have a common purpose—to go to the source of thought, to that deep essence of our very being. The idea is to let go of all the debris, called thoughts, that drifts by on the river of awareness. As we do so, the mind floats down to the depth of the stream and gets in touch with the infinite, un-bounded stillness from which all of this stuff called life arises. The many different vehicles of meditation are there to support you in becoming less attached to the thoughts, the debris floating on the surface. Therefore, it is natural in the meditation process to let even the vehicle of meditation fade or change as it will. Meditation be-comes a powerful teaching of "letting go and letting God."

Just as you don't try to make your body heal, meditation practice isn't about trying to get rid of unwanted thoughts. Nor is it about subjectively analyzing what goes on in your mind during meditation. For example, if I ask you to close your eyes and then I say, "Don't think of pink elephants," what is the first thing that comes to your mind? The medium of the mind is thoughts. Fighting or judging or resisting thoughts in meditation is struggling against the mind's natu-ral process.

Meditation can be a powerful stress-releasing process. When the mind/body reaches a state of deep relaxation through meditation, deeply held tensions are released. The body readjusts itself at a cellular level, and mentally this release of energy shows up as a stream of thoughts. Thoughts that occur during meditation are there-fore a by-product of stress release. They are not the stress release themselves. The release has already happened on a deep physiolog-ical level. Knowing this, we can let the thoughts go, as they are like clouds passing over on a sunny day. At certain times we may be-come absorbed in them. They may be trivial or heavy. That's OK. I think of thoughts as a rerun of an old movie. Maybe it's a melodrama one moment and a comedy the next. It doesn't matter. The thoughts can simply pass by when we rest our attention on the vehicle of meditation that we are using. We can surrender and take it as it comes. The universe knows what we need and will provide it. Medi-tation is about trust.

Another pitfall is the tendency to subjectively analyze the medita-tion during the process. When we don't have our expectations met, we might become frustrated. Perhaps we once had an incredible experience with meditation and want to repeat it. Or we have read about what meditation is supposed to be and we try to reproduce that. The secret is to be comfortable with ourselves and know that all we have to do is surrender to that deep essence, to the universe itself.

I have found that when meditation is done on a regular basis, a valuable habit will be built up quickly. We are meditating to bring up that deep, submerged essence of our self into everyday life so that its power and serenity permeate every activity. Habitual meditation is like taking a cloth and putting it in dye and then laying it out in the sun to bleach out. And then putting it back into the dye, and back and forth until little by little the cloth gets a deeper and more permanent color. What is important is the daily process of bringing the essence of your being out and putting it into the world. And then putting it back. The world becomes more vivid and you become more vital, responsible, and effective in it.

We have an opportunity to explore and to discover for ourselves the ability to go within. Ask questions and have the courage to admit vulnerability and uncertainty in learning a new technique for improving your life. Follow your own heart regarding the choice of a meditation technique. Most of all, enjoy. That's what precious gifts are for.

## LETTING GO

Letting go is never easy when we are holding on to something we consider precious. And yet, often it is exactly what we need to do.

---

*There was a man hanging from a cliff two thousand feet above the valley floor. The terrified man looked to the top of the cliff and screamed, "Is there anyone up there who can help me?"*

*A deep, booming reply came from above, "Yes, I'll help you. I'm the Lord. Just relax and let go."*

*A long pause.*

*"Is there anybody else up there who can help me?"*

---

Letting go sounds so simple until the time comes to actually do it. It takes trust and an understanding that you are not alone but exist as an interdependent being, connected to the world around you. In Aiki workshops, participants experience increased power and strength when they let go of physical tension. A similar feeling emerges as we let go of our other attachments, whether they be emotional, material, or philosophical. Trust means being willing to let go of all attachments. It is being totally free. To be truly secure, we must be absolutely vulnerable.

In the early 1970s, aikido master Koichi Tohei of Japan came to our Aspen Academy of Martial Arts in Colorado to teach a special class in aikido and *ki* (energy) development. Koichi Tohei had been one of founder Ueshiba's prize *uchideshi* (live-in students) for many years before the Founder appointed him Chief Instructor of the Art of Aikido. When he came to our academy in the Rocky Mountains, he was going through one of the most difficult conflicts of his life. He was making a decision to leave his position as Chief Instructor and to start his own new school and style of aikido. To do this in the martial arts community was tantamount to treason. He would have to break completely from any association with the Founder's original school.

Sensitive to his internal turmoil, I invited Master Tohei to go for a long drive in the mountains to a majestic setting known as the Maroon Bells—fourteen-thousand-foot peaks paternally watching over a crystal-clear lake. Certainly a centered environment for clarity and understanding. Over the next few hours, Master Tohei spoke honestly and frankly.

"Whenever I have trouble, I must center myself. I have great trust when I am centered. I have been in great conflict over whether or not to leave Hombu [the aikido headquarters in Tokyo]. Yet when I am centered, things become very clear. I must go. I trust myself absolutely when I am centered."

I asked him how he came to have such trust in the appropriateness of his decisions and why this quality called centering was the foundation of all of his teachings. He mentioned Ueshiba's teachings and demonstrations as big factors in his appreciation for this quality. To see a little (ninety-eight pounds) man in his late eighties control several large strong men effortlessly certainly would get anyone's attention. In Master Tohei's case, however, the actual integration of this powerful state called centering had come as a result of his experience in World War II.

"I spent several years serving my country and leading a band of Japanese soldiers deep into China during our invasion of that country. I was convinced then of the rightness of *O Sensei*'s [great teacher

—the title of reverence historically given to Master Ueshiba] teaching that we should have peaceful, loving attitudes toward all beings and was committed to discovering a way to reconcile my position in the army with that philosophy. I realized the common element of both was that it was my job to protect my men. What better way to do that than not to harm anyone else!"

Before he could instill this philosophy in his men, however, Tohei realized he needed to earn their respect. He looked younger than his years and that added to the difficulty. During their first skirmish, Tohei got an idea. Since all the men were taking cover in trenches, he felt it would be an obvious display of courage (although the word *crazy* kept coming up in my mind as I listened) not to duck down into the trench but to remain standing and call orders powerfully. To do this he would need great trust in his center, to distinguish between courage and stupidity. He would get centered and stand up. His men couldn't believe his actions.

"When I lost my center and could not get it back immediately, I would go down. But I had definitely earned their respect."

During the entire time Koichi Tohei was in China, none of his men were killed. He attributed this to their never injuring an enemy.

"When we did capture an enemy, instead of sending him back to our headquarters I would untie his hands at night and tell him to leave. We did not wish to harm him. There were times during the war when we would be moving along a road and the enemy would recognize us from a hill in the distance. Instead of firing at us, it was as if they were waving at us to go on in peace, which we did."

Master Tohei also described how he would use the same centering technique to decide where to go. If he lost his feeling of centeredness, he would immediately recapture it. But if he wasn't able to do so, he would change direction and proceed to repeat the centering test.

"It may sound crazy to most people, but I never lost a man. It worked."

As Master Tohei looked at the serene mountain lake and the majestic peaks around him, a bright smile emerged on his face. It was clear he had let go of the inner turmoil and trusted his centered decision to change the course of his life.

## CENTERED RELATIONSHIPS

In workshops, I am often asked, "If it is possible to be centered on an individual basis, can we also choose to have our relationships be centered?" Good question. What does a centered relationship look like, and how is it different from the relationships we have now?

Knowing the power of learning through experience, I ask for a volunteer. I have him stand with feet shoulder-width apart, bend over at the waist, and "walk out" with his hands until he is evenly supporting himself by both hands and feet. Once he has created this "arched bridge," I stand facing him, perpendicular to him, gently allowing my body to lean over his back as if he were a horse packing a dead soldier. I ask mischievously, "Do you know any relationships that look like this one?" For most, the question hits uncomfortably close to home.

By now I'm completely collapsed over my friend's back and he is straining under the burden. I inquire of the other participants, "For whom do you think the conflict is more uncomfortable, me or my partner?"

Most participants see the strain in my partner's body and face and give him the vote. They can all relate to the great weight of responsibility, literally having to carry another person. It is also evident in this graphic demonstration that my partner has the added worry of knowing that if he ever lets go of the struggle, both of us could be injured in the collapse resulting from his failure to handle the "responsibility."

"But what about me?" I protest, looking more scared and helpless at the possibility of falling. "Have you ever been in a relationship in which your stability and happiness were dependent upon another person?" When this happens, the dependent partner operates out of fear and helplessness. He must constantly manipulate the other to be sure that everything stays as it is, or their lives will collapse under them.

The difficulty of a dependent relationship becomes obvious. What usually results is that the person bearing the weight grows more angry, while the fear of loss or change increases in the other. Each side becomes resentful and needs to get back at the other. The typical outcome is that they agree, usually unconsciously, to reverse the role (I get on all fours and my partner collapses over me) and the pattern repeats. Sound familiar?

"Let's experience a centered relationship." My partner and I stand back to back, or shoulder to shoulder. We lean gently into one another to feel the support, but do so from a centered place. We reach out and gently test each other's center in this new position. The choreography of support becomes clear to the workshop participants. There is an increased feeling of comfort and stability and a real acknowledgment of the support that each is receiving, but there is also an understanding that the stability and balance of each individual is not dependent upon the other. We certainly use and appreciate the support, but if one person were to leave or change the form of the relationship for a period of time, the other person would not be devastated. Adjustments may need to be made, but the fearful anxiety brought on by the possibility of collapse would not occur.

Powerful relationships arise when two centered individuals commit themselves to unconditionally love one another and to support each other's growth toward their full potential. Both give freely, without selfish motives or the desire to lock the relationship into any particular form. There are no boundaries when we fully embrace each other.

*If your happiness depends on what somebody else does ... you do have a problem.*
Richard Bach

## CENTERED ENVIRONMENT

In this chapter, we have focused on centering within the individual and its effect on relationships. However, we are also an integral part of our environment and are deeply affected by the culture in which we live. Our progress in understanding centering and actually being centered can be greatly influenced by what is going on around us. This is true for establishing any new habits. It's a lot tougher to establish healthy eating habits if you work in a junk food restaurant, or to free yourself of an alcohol addiction if you work in a bar.

Ideally, a centered environment is one that supports you in becoming more relaxed, in thinking clearly, and in reminding you in positive and nurturing ways of your vision, purpose, and goals in life. The way you have chosen to set up your home is a good reflection of this. Factors such as noise, clutter, cleanliness, and even color choice affect your living. Tests show that rooms decorated in bright oranges, yellows, and reds tend to bring up the level of excitement, while blues and greens help create a calm and soothing feeling. Either is appropriate, depending on the outcome you desire.

Good physical health is part of a centered environment. Placing nutrition and fitness as high priorities in our lives works wonders on our self-esteem, helping us to lead more positive and productive lives. What kind of food do you have right now in your refrigerator and cupboards? How educated are you about proper diet? How is your weight and muscle tone for your age? What about heart rate, cholesterol level? What habits do you have that you would like to reduce or eliminate?

A critical aspect of creating a centered environment is to consciously choose as friends and associates those people who are committed, inspirational, and powerfully active. Astonishing results can be attained simply by "modeling" or imitating the behavior of those we would like to emulate. Since we have this capability, why not choose as compatriots those we feel are models of excellence and not mediocrity?

If you are active in the world, you certainly will find yourself among those with whom you would not normally associate. But if the critical mass—the core group around you—are people who have a positive effect on you, then you will more readily be able to uplift and inspire others who are operating from fear and negativity, instead of being pulled down as a result of your associations with them. Centered environments are your choice. If you make that choice daily, you create a thermal, making soaring and gliding upward a joyful reality.

There are many ways to help create a more centered environment in the home. Taking responsibility to see that your family has adequate rest, excellent nutrition, and lots of choices for exercise and fitness will go far in support of a more centered environment. Providing choices for stimulating the mind and creativity will do more to naturally curtail excessive boob-tube time than a lot of suggestions to turn it off. Having regular times when the members of a household can be together without other distractions, such as sit-down meals and group meetings, will add to the security and stability of a home. The establishment of a quiet place for working, meditating/praying, or relaxing in silence is usually greatly appreciated. More importantly, as you become more centered and excited by life, everyone around you will be influenced in a positive manner.

Getting the employees together in non-work-related activities has proven invaluable in creating a more effective and centered workplace. Regular and planned group activities such as sporting events, guest lectures on non-work-related subjects, and social gatherings do much to eliminate tension and increase *esprit de corps*. The workplace also can benefit from a quiet room where people can relax and regather their personal resources. The availability of health snacks versus junk food snacks, fitness breaks versus smoking breaks, wellness days versus sick days, and celebration meetings vs. "crisis" meetings will greatly enhance efficiency, effectiveness, and happiness. All of these ideas are best nurtured by centered individuals who are living models of doing them rather than just talking about them.

Successful business people and CEO's know the value of a centered environment. Klaus Obermeyer, of the internationally known Obermeyer line of skiwear and equipment, is a man who leads by example. Instead of holing up in an executive office, Klaus is everywhere in the plant, laughing, smiling, and encouraging people. "It's all attitude. I love what I do and one of the most important things a leader can do is to let that joy out. It's contagious." Knowing the value of fitness, he installed a solar-heated swimming pool for employees of his plant in Aspen, Colorado. And it doesn't go unused. Klaus himself leads the way, swimming at least one thousand meters each day.

William Farley, who owns one of the nation's largest privately held industrial corporations, with sales nearing $2 billion per year, is another good example. Soon after acquiring a new plant, Farley will poll workers to find out what kind of athletic facility they would like. Baseball fields, tracks, horeshoe pits, tennis courts, exercise rooms staffed with experts, and even a golf-driving booth provide Farley

Industries employees with the opportunity to improve their health and fitness levels and control stress. This in turn benefits the company through low absentee rates, a lower employee turnover, a low back-log of union grievances, and decreased health care costs.

The best influence you can have on your environment—actually, the highest gift you can give others—is the quality of your own being. As you choose to be centered, your heightened awareness will naturally lead to a more appropriate environment. As you change in positive ways, people begin to notice, to ask questions, and to model themselves after you more and more.

# WINDSTAR

Millions of people the world over are familiar with the music of John Denver. His songs of the heart connect people of all nations with the common threads of humanity, family, hard work, sensitivity to children, and the environment. He has become a powerful global spokesperson for peace and has long recognized the need for a centered environment.

In the midseventies, I began working with John on the art of aikido and on meditation. John and I would stay up late at night after concerts on the road, swapping perspectives about life. We found that we shared, among other things, a dream of a place where people could come and experience the things he sang about—harmony with the earth and each other. It was, admittedly, a lofty ideal, but one day we decided we would actually create that place. The idea of Windstar was born. Shortly thereafter, we found ourselves on one thousand acres of exquisite land high in the Rocky Mountains. Its boundaries are delineated by mountains and form the shape of a great whale. In 1978, Windstar found a home.

The next six years were devoted to defining what Windstar was, both in terms of vision and physical manifestation. We built a large freeform tent in which to conduct Aiki classes and other workshops. We put up a circle of tipis to house workshop participants; we built solar showers, a wood-burning sauna and hot tub, and composting toilets. We dug four large ponds and created a large, diverse garden to feed participants. The land is used for research in food-growing technologies such as bio-intensive growing methods and Windstar's unique Biodome, a structure developed with Buckminster Fuller to grow produce and raise fish efficiently year round. We proved that things can grow beautifully year round, even at an altitude of seven thousand feet, where the average outdoor growing season is sixty days a year. We turned the upper acres into a wildlife preserve and set a meditation tipi there in full view of Mount Sopris, sacred to the Ute Indians. We renovated the existing ranchhouse with state-of-the-art energy technologies, including a smorgasbord of solar devices and a large wind generator for electricity and back-up hot water heating. Programs whose subjects ranged from Aiki to aquaculture were begun.

Participants in the Windstar Aiki workshops come for a week's stay. We are awakened in the morning by a bell and proceed in silence to meditation and breathing classes in the tent. A warm, healthy breakfast and good company break the silence, and the rest of the day is spent studying, eating homegrown meals, meditating, and exercising the mind and body. Participants experience a centered environment. Is it the trappings of the facility that do it?

The truth is, there are countless problems going on at any point in time at Windstar. The composting toilets are a good trek from bed. The weather can turn cold. The solar showers aren't always hot. There always seems to be a skunk in the neighborhood. Those with a sweet tooth can't buy a sweet roll or Hershey bar to save their lives. The bell often comes too early; the evening bonfire smoke gets in your eyes. The "state-of-the-art" solar technologies have become museum pieces compared to what is available today. And the tipis sometimes leak.

The amazing thing is that the participants find, after a week of living at Windstar, a special joy, a serenity and a reacquaintance with their spiritual sides. They feel more aware. They come closer in touch with their potential. They like themselves more. All this *in spite* of the skunks, cold showers, and leaks. In a centered environment, the facility, the land, and the trappings are important, but the attitude of the people is the critical ingredient.

## THE GENTLE TOUCH

All the sanctuaries, fitness spas, and fruit smoothies in the world won't create a centered environment for one who is determined to be malcontent. It's *our choice*.

Since most of us live in nowhere near an ideal environment, we need to diligently promote positive changes in our culture without creating unnecessary and stressful resistance in the process. Many of us have had the negative experience of a close friend who has just undergone some major change in his thinking and become an "evangelical pest," speaking of nothing but his new religion, vitamin, exercise program, or guru, to the point where we feel guilty and angry and frantically search for a bag to tie over his head. We wonder, who is this strange alien disguised as our friend and pretending to be a mother, father, and priest all rolled into one insensitive authority?

As we become enthusiastic about something new of great value to ourselves, there is an initial tendency to keep persuading ourselves of the validity of it. Unfortunately, our method of doing this often seems to involve persuading someone else. So off we go on our "mission from God." We proceed up our friends' sidewalks, wondering why we hear doors being bolted and window shades dropping.

I cringe when I hear of people leaving some beneficial workshop or training, all pumped up with the great value they've received and the new skills they've learned, walking into their homes to unsuspecting, innocent family members, and declaring something like, "OK, it's 5:30! Everyone turn off the TV and stereo and stop talking for the next half hour. *I'm* going to meditate." The unspoken message communicated is "I'm spiritual, you're not. I'm right, you're wrong. It's too bad you don't know what I know." All the stress that these people thought they had the skills to eliminate comes back in even greater doses.

Years ago I returned from a three-month meditation retreat in the Swiss Alps, where I was doing very intensive work on myself and eating healthy vegetarian meals. I emerged from my "cave" on Christmas Eve and returned to the United States, to a traditional

Christmas dinner at my parents' home with all the relatives present. There I sat, in front of a ham and turkey dinner with all the trimmings. I opened my mouth and began, "I discovered during my retreat that eating—"

I stopped in midsentence as I noticed the sudden silence in the room. Fortunately I had the clarity of mind to scan the table of relatives and settle my gaze on my mother, looking so loving and radiant, as all moms do when surrounded by their brood on festive occasions. This was truly a centered environment. I recognized as of that moment that if I were to proceed with my righteous food lecture about the benefits of not eating meat, I would do more damage to my digestive system (not to mention others'), by negating the love that had gone into this food, than if I consumed a case of Alpo. I quickly completed my sentence with a newly discovered truth, "—eating and being at home with people who love you is the best possible nutrition around." Whew! A lot of unnecessary stress avoided. Feeling very centered and loved, I enjoyed two helpings of everything and felt great afterwards.

Consciously creating a supportive environment for nurturing a lifestyle that is positive, powerful, and in alignment with our true purpose takes awareness and action. And it is well worth the effort.

## Risk Takers

*Why not go out on a limb? That's where the fruit is.*
Will Rogers

A lawyer friend of mine was convinced that his clients were paying more attention to the exterior than the interior—i.e., to how they thought he was supposed to look and sound rather than the content of his counsel. He decided that for one day he would meet, greet, and counsel in his old blue bathrobe. This friend was a risk taker.

Art Buchwald tells of a friend who made it his job to bring love back to New York City by complimenting everyone—from cabbies to skyscraper builders—on jobs well done. His theory was that if out of ten people he met he could make three happy, these would, in turn, spread goodwill and influence the attitudes of three thousand more in one day.

One day Art saw his friend wink at a very plain-looking woman and called him on that.

"Yes, I know," said the friend. "And if she's a schoolteacher, her class will be in for a fantastic day."[8]

These people are risk takers, and I invite you to be one, too.

As an alternative to the traditional self-help assignments that you would probably disregard anyway, here are some happy, although perhaps zany, hints to playing with common daily experiences and conflicts in a totally different manner. These are risks, but they are also good for you. Aim for a loving, learning attitude when you try them out. In any case, they will certainly prevent boredom, allow for fresh insights, and provide excellent opportunities for practicing centering.

- At certain times you may have to put up with someone who treats you disdainfully or rudely, because he is in charge of some bureaucratic task that you have to fulfill, such as obtaining a driver's license or going through customs. He may even say "No" to something you want, or make you late. As you feel those daggers appearing before your eyes, get centered and see that person as some distant relative, some long-lost brother or sister. Smile and thank him for doing a conscientious job. If you have to return at some point later on, give him a gift, like a cookie or a flower—sincerely, not cynically. After all, that person is your long-lost brother.

- Try this with the traffic cop or state patrol officer who stops you to give you a ticket. After all, he deserves a compliment for doing his job. Or compliment the referee officiating a game in which you played, even if you lost.

- When you're dealing with a person who is extremely angry, and his or her attitude is beginning to affect your calmness, shift your perspective of that person. Visualize a carrot in his ear as he is talking to you, or mentally change the clothing he has on. Put him in clothing of an entirely different era, like that of a court jester or perhaps a samurai warrior with the ludicrous addition of a child's rubber sword in his hand in place of the real thing.

• When you're having one of those frustrating times trying to get through on the telephone, get centered and picture the operator as someone who is there all day on the phone willing to help you. Thank her. Tell her to have a nice day. Acknowledge her willingness to help you and compliment her on her pleasant-sounding voice or unusual persistence.

• Go into your kitchen and take out of your refrigerator and cupboards any food items that you feel you would like to eliminate from your diet. This might include foods with excess saccharin, sugar, salt, caffeine, or cholesterol. Throw them in the garbage. Change your eating habits this very day, for your lifetime.

• Ever notice how everyone in an elevator stares up at the floor light indicators? The next time you find yourself in a crowded elevator—turn around and face the people. Remain calm and centered and quiet as you look into their eyes. Do not try to make people uncomfortable by staring. Yet let go of your own fear of continuing if some discomfort does arise. Upon leaving, give them a hearty yet truthful farewell such as "Nice being with you." (Even if you never try this, I'll bet you think of it whenever you ride on an elevator! The thought alone can center you.)

---

**THE AIKI APPROACH**
**Choose to Be Centered**

Being centered:

—is a psychophysiological state that is strengthened through practice;

—allows you to be more authentic, sensitive, and open;

—produces emotional and physical stability;

—has a positive effect on relationships and the surrounding environment;

—has great impact in developing trust;

—enables you to appreciate the nature of conflict;

—brings you to a point of clarity, the point of power;

—is always your choice, at *any* time.

*Embrace Tiger, Return to Mountain*
Old Chinese Saying

# 5. Accept Your Connectedness

*It was a beautiful, harmonious, peaceful-looking planet, blue with white clouds, and one that gave you a deep sense . . . of home, of being, of identity. It is what I prefer to call instant global connectedness.*

Edgar Mitchell
Astronaut, viewing earth from the moon

At our annual Windstar symposium on "Choices for the Future," astronaut Rusty Schweickart, the first American to "free" spacewalk without a tether, was showing breathtaking slides of his "walk." He described himself gazing down upon the Earth while hanging onto a ladder outside his spacecraft, which happened to be moving at seventeen thousand miles per hour (with no wind, mind you).

---

We know that the earth is round. We know there are people on it. We know that they are all like us. But when you fly around it time and time again—90 minutes to get around the whole earth—again and again and again, it comes in a different way. It doesn't come in through the head. It comes in through the heart, in through the gut. When you come down from that experience, you've crossed thousands and thousands of borders and boundaries that are artificially created. They work nice on maps. You paint them orange and blue and green. But that's not what it is when viewed from space. You don't even see those boundaries and borders. We created them, guys, and it's up to us to do something about it. I'd suggest that this perspective is one that might help a little bit in taking responsibility for this planet as a whole and for all the life on it. That's what comes through to you when you're up there in space, when you're flying around this beautiful planet.[9]

This man was not talking just philosophically. He had been there, and it was obvious that his experience of deep connectedness with the earth had transformed him permanently. You could see the love and compassion for his earth in his clear eyes and purposeful body movements, in the sound of his voice, and in the conviction of his words. Moreover, the deep connection that he felt was contagious. The thousand-plus people in the audience began to feel bonded to Mother Earth and to the intimate nature of our relationship with her.

To demonstrate simply the principle of connectedness when I do workshops on conflict resolution, I draw a curved line on the blackboard.

I ask the audience if they can see that the drawing is a concave line. Many respond, "Yes, that's right. Of course." I then stand to the left of the line and declare fervently, "No! Absolutely not! This is a convex line." I then leap to the right, stating, "Excuse me, Sir, but I can prove to you that this line is concave." I proceed to hop back and forth from one side of the line to the other, making right and true statements about my position, one moment proving "convexity," the next proving "concavity." The audience understands quickly the lunacy of it all. It's not a concave line. It's not a convex line. It's a concave/convex line by definition. The two qualities are connected and exist only with each other. A half cup of water is seen by some as half full and others as half empty.

How often have you been in an argument and spent most of your time and energy trying to be right, trying to prove your position, while the other person was trying just as fervently to prove hers? Neither of you is listening because each is so engrossed in articulating his or her proofs. You see only differences, and the more "right" each of you strives to be, the more separate you become and the more limited your ability becomes to resolve the conflict.

Yet, as in the curved line example, the reality is that we are connected just by being in conflict with one another. Separation is an illusion. Connectedness is real. Have you ever had a serious fight with your children or your parents? You could move thousands of miles away. Would the separation resolve your conflict? Rarely. Increasing your connectedness, recognizing and welcoming your relatedness to the world and the people around you, will always support the resolution of a conflict.

When Samantha Smith, a thirteen-year-old girl from Maine, became dismayed at the lack of friendship between the United States and the Soviet Union, she sent a simple handwritten letter to Leonid Brezhnev, General Secretary of the Soviet Union in 1982. Her strong desire to create a relationship between our two nations sparked a positive Soviet-American citizen-diplomacy program at a critical time in a very cold war. She became an international spokesperson for peace. The momentum from the actions of such a compassionate and peace-loving youth did much to resolve our fears and increase our hopes about cooperative possibilities between the two nations. When she died suddenly in a plane crash at the age of sixteen, she was mourned as much in the Soviet Union as in the United States.

Fred Smith, founder of Federal Express, was disturbed when one of his cargo terminals could not keep things running on time. Instead of seeing the conflict as a right/wrong situation and reacting by immediately blaming or firing people, he decided to examine connections. Upon investigating, he learned that it was in the employees' interest to work less efficiently and run late because it meant they made more money. In order to connect and blend with this interest, he gave them all a minimum guarantee and said, "Look, if you get through before a certain time, just go home. You will have beat the system." Within a few weeks, the deliveries were way ahead of schedule and the employees made just as much money and had more time off.[10]

What would it be like if you could increase your connectedness with anyone—your child, boss, friends, or parents—at any time, by expanding your power, your energy, your field of influence? When we see Jacques Cousteau on TV sharing a magic moment underwater, we can't help but experience his total connection with and love for the ocean. We become deeply aware of the absurdity of treating our precious life support, water, as a disposable commodity. His personal connection with the ocean is so strong that even though we are watching a TV show filmed thousands of miles away, we become more committed to doing our part to protect our vital oceans. When coach Vince Lombardi walked onto a football field, "even the ball sat up." The Green Bay Packers organization was made up of individuals, but his personal power of connectedness was such that a team emerged, as if by magic. The players, coaches—even the fans—gave total commitment to team play and produced some of the greatest football teams in history.

Let's examine this kind of energy and power within ourselves and our ability to express it.

The fundamental unit of energy in life is called *ki* in Japan and *chi* in China. In Hollywood, George Lucas dramatized it as "The Force" in his Star Wars epics, and it was an essential element in their popular appeal. We may not be able to move spaceships with our minds, but we have all heard of a small woman lifting a car to save a child, or of similar remarkable performances occurring in emergencies or in the intensity of sporting events. Most of us think these feats happen only in times of crisis or under other unusual circumstances.

Yet this energy is all around us every day, and we can learn to recognize it and connect with it at any time. When a baby grasps your finger, you are apt to remark how incredibly strong her grip is. That baby knows nothing about our concepts of strength. She isn't tense or desperate and her grip is in no way painful. Only when you try to unwrap her fingers from yours do you recognize the power of her connectedness. The baby has simply and naturally "welded" the energy of her hand and your finger and is quite content to have things that way. It feels good. There is no conflict in her mind about being strong enough or too strong.

Pick that baby up and lay her across your outstretched palm on her stomach; she won't flop over your hand like a wet dishrag. Her entire body will be naturally extended horizontally, as if it were one unit of energy. When you lift her by her feet when she is lying on her back, her entire body will rise as one unit rather than separate at the waist like the bodies of most adults. These aren't just powers of infancy that disappear with age and greater size, but examples of *ki* extension—unconsciously practicing connectedness within one's body and with the world around us. There are *ki* development exercises that can teach us how to attain this optimum psychophysiological state whenever we choose.

# THE ENERGY ARM

One of my favorite *ki* development exercises is "the unbendable arm."[11] Extend your arm straight out in front of you and have a friend of equal or greater physical strength try to bend it at the elbow by pulling down on your biceps with one hand and pushing your wrist up with the other, applying a constantly increasing pressure, not a jerky motion. Inevitably, if you are conditioned like the great majority of people on the planet today, you will clench your fist, grit your teeth and tense up your whole arm, prepared to resist his force by using force directly against him. By applying the proper leverage, he will be able to bend your arm after a few moments. The pain and discomfort of trying to overcome his power by straining, clenching and tensing will be too much for you to endure for very long.

Now, imagine your center as an infinite reservoir of water and your arm as no longer a physical arm but a fire hose, as large around as you would like. Your fingers become the nozzle of the fire hose. First, put *no* water in the hose (i.e., let your arm go limp) and have your partner attempt to bend it. No problem. Then, as you did in the try-to-be-strong-through-tension example, put "ice" in the hose, as if it had been left outside in subfreezing weather, and have your partner try to bend it again. With enough pressure, the ice will "break" and your arm will suddenly bend.

Finally, turn on that infinite supply of water from your center and allow it to spray out your finger-nozzle. Let your fingers wave easily back and forth to insure that your muscles don't tense up inadvertently. Relax your shoulder and visualize the stream of water flowing out from the center, up through your body, and out through your shoulder and arm. Keep your elbow slightly bent, not locked. Watch the water spraying out from your extended fingers as far as you can conceptualize—through walls, trees, mountains, people.

Just as a fully turned-on fire hose is pliable, yet unbendable and unbreakable, your arm will stay soft to the touch, giving a little but not breaking down because of the external pressure. Your arm is now connected to your own center and to the world through flowing energy. To bend it, your partner has to contend not with a few muscle fibers, but with an unlimited river of energy.

As energy effortlessly flows out from your center, you, in your great comfort and ease, may notice that your friend is sweating and grunting and straining to no avail. The typical response from this state of true power, of energy flowing freely, is "Oh come on. You're not really trying to bend my arm, are you?"

Throughout the world, I have had my workshop participants perform this simple exercise. It is fascinating to watch large, masculine men react in disbelief as they see their patterned response to what they *think* is power and strength crumble before their eyes. They discover that even greater power and strength is available with much less effort.

Whether I'm working with professional athletes, police officers, business people, or politicians, the transformation is just as revealing. As soon as they experience that there is power and strength in responses other than those of tension and struggle, their thinking about the possibility of peace in the world undergoes a major shift. Their image of peace moves from one of passivity and weakness (as in the limp arm example) to one of true power and strength and vitality (the open, flowing-energy arm). To be able to let go of our culture's fixation on the forceful, adversarial approach (the war state) as the only method appropriate during a crisis requires that people experience alternatives that contain great power and vitality.

Christ, Gandhi, and Dr. Martin Luther King, Jr., were powerful, not weak; active, not passive. They were maximally effective in their environment and culture. Their *ki* was continually extending, connecting, and influencing all those around them. This ability to be an effective peacemaker can be learned and integrated into *your* experience and *your* daily life. When a conflict arises, you have the ability to establish that energized and connected state *now*. As a result, all sides in a conflict feel more connected, with greater rapport and an increased sense of cooperation.

## THE ENERGY SPHERE

Have you ever walked into your home, classroom, or office and sensed a heaviness or a troublesome atmosphere even though no one has said anything out of the ordinary or acted any differently? You may have had the experience of walking into the living room of your home, with your upset mate three rooms away, and sensed the impending doom in the air as powerfully as if it were written in neon lights. You sense conflict looming ahead and anxiety begins creeping in—you loosen your necktie or open the window to create more space. What is your typical reaction to this sudden drop in the relationship barometer? Is it the guilt-ridden thought "Uh oh, what did I do now?" or maybe the "Get them before they get me" approach "Yeah, well I'm angry too because . . ."?

We are indeed energy beings as well as physical bodies. The energy field around us changes as we change—emotionally, spiritually, and physiologically. The reverse is also true. Our psychophysiological states are affected by the energy field around us, and there appear to be no limits to our ability to change and affect this field.

A simple yet profound way to experience the effect of the relationship between connectedness and conflict is to think of the energy field around you as a large sphere. This *ki* sphere can contract or expand like a balloon. When you are upset, angry, or scared, this energy balloon naturally contracts. It's like running back into a fortress, barring the doors, and slamming shut the windows, fearful because you may be under siege at any moment. On the other hand, when you are full of joy, confidence, or compassion, the ball of *ki* around you grows and expands. All windows and doors are open to give out from and to receive into. You look and feel different, not just to yourself but to others.

All conflicts, in fact all relationships, can be seen as contraction and expansion phenomena.[12] And the knowledge and skill of being able to expand your *ki* sphere or connectedness *now* provides you with a powerful condition with which to resolve conflicts. Without this knowledge, we tend to play the victim, and unconsciously fall into old patterned reactions of negativity.

Let's say you walk into your office one morning and your colleague Gertrude is in a very sour, "Don't even look at me the wrong way or I'll knock your block off" mood. You look around—there is no one else in the office. No escape. It's *mano a mano*, survival of the toughest. Too bad for Gertrude. Or you. Or both.

Assuming that you arrived in a positive mood yourself, with *ki* extended, what has happened to your energy sphere? Your defensive reaction has shrunk in to "protect" your center from her bad mood, and as a result, you feel contracted and depressed. "It's not my fault," you may say to yourself as you slink into your own corner, feeling as if you actually *had* done something wrong and blaming Gertrude for the whole mess.

We are often patterned to deal with contraction around us by contracting. It's a reaction. We do it unconsciously. If you contract, what do you think Gertrude's tendency is? To feel more separated and to contract some more. The process of contraction and depression continues, until with enough contraction on both sides, we literally disappear from each other's lives. And we wonder why relationships end? When those walls (really our own energy "space") are contracting around us, depressing us, we react to this prison in a variety of ways: lethargy, boredom, sadness, agitation, anger, and hatred.

But when you are aware of this contraction/expansion phenomenon of relationships, you realize that you have a choice about your *ki* field and that you have the ability to affect it at any time. Radically different possibilities emerge. You are able to take responsibility for the conflict and effectively create the atmosphere needed for its resolution. You recognize Gertrude's upset more objectively as what it is—a contraction of energy. Instead of placing blame or spending your energy on negative reactions, you simply expand your *ki* sphere to fill the gap left by her contraction. You lose nothing. In fact, both of you gain.

Gertrude will feel the positive effect of your *ki* expansion. It will counteract the negative emotional effect of her own contraction. Her natural tendency will be to expand as she feels heard or appreciated or accepted regardless of her present state. Connectedness and rapport will replace estrangement and hostility.

Your personal interaction with Gertrude can take on many different forms, depending on the situation and the closeness of your relationship. The essential thing is to keep extending your energy to include her and to act in a way you feel is appropriate. That may be sitting down next to her and asking if there is anything troubling her that you can help with. You can communicate your appreciation and acknowledgment of her feelings and her problem.

"Tough morning, huh? That's all right. If you want to go out for a cup of coffee, go ahead. I'll be in my office if you need me."

You may simply smile and act warmly to express understanding. Or you may choose not to intervene with her at all and simply go on about your business while including her in your *ki* field. Perhaps a distraction is in order—you can engage her in a conversation about a mutual interest outside the office or a topic about which you know she is positive and enthusiastic. You can say something funny or do something outrageously silly, like stepping in the wastebasket—any number of things that would interrupt her present physiological pattern.

Each of these actions can be just as inappropriate as appropriate. The form must emerge from the quality of your own being, your own *ki* field—something that is "you," not from some prearranged strategy based on what you think you ought to do in such a situation. Designed strategies may be effective, but only if a state of connectedness, rapport, and trust has been established.

Our favorite schoolteachers are adept at expanding their *ki* spheres to include every child in the class. Let's say Miss Jones sees Billy, her new fourth-grade pupil, arrive for his first day full of fear and disapproval. She has a choice: Will she feel his negativity and contract because she takes it as a personal threat? Or will she expand her *ki* sphere, taking him in with reassurances, sensitivity, and a smile? In such an atmosphere of acceptance, instruction and correction can take place without anyone being made to feel wrong or humiliated for making mistakes.

When we choose to respond with a feeling of connectedness and positive energy to short-tempered salesclerks, frustrated waiters, nearsighted referees, and slow drivers, everybody's day is brighter.

## POLISHING THE MIRROR

How is your breathing like your life? The following is an exercise that will greatly help you in developing your *ki*, in order to increase your vitality and power and to assist your growing clarity and connectedness with the world around you.

- Stand centered, with feet at least shoulder-width apart.
- Bend the knees as if sitting in a chair, with back remaining straight. The "height" of the imagined seat is your choice. The more you bend your knees, the more you may have to widen your stance to keep your back straight. Adjust the width of stance and the degree of knee-bend so that you feel balanced and strongly connected to the earth.
- When you are in this seated position, place your hands together in front of your abdomen with palms facing away from you, as if you were placing them on a window.
- Inhaling slowly and deeply from your center through your nostrils, allow your body to rise in the same slow pace as your inhalation until you are in a standing position. Continue to raise the hands until they are extended comfortably above head level, palms still flat on the window. The time it takes to do this should be the time it takes to make a full inhalation.
- Let your breath settle powerfully into every aspect of your body, as your hands spread out, slightly more than shoulder width apart. The exact width of the spread will vary with the individual. Let your awareness be on the power and energy building at your center. Even though you are not inhaling or exhaling during this settling, it is not a tense "holding." You are instead allowing the energy to flow into and heal every cell. The *ki* of life always flows, never stopping or holding.
- The exhalation is made slowly and powerfully through the mouth. Allowing the breath to make a continuous sound (by opening your mouth as if you were saying *ha*) will enable you to monitor the flow of breath and to keep it continuous.

- As you are exhaling, return to the "squat" position. Exhale fully and completely, releasing all tension. The range of movement will vary with the individual and may change as you feel more relaxed and flexible.
- During the transition between exhalation and inhalation, your hands slowly come back together with palms still flat against the window. Your mouth easily closes and another inhalation begins, smoothly and gently.

The visualization that will assist you in comfort and in developing strong *ki* is that of cleaning your windows of perception. With each inhalation, the energy of the universe is coming into your entire body and mind, healing and energizing each cell and allowing you to see the world fresh and new. You are embracing the entire universe and becoming one with it. Upon exhalation, you are erasing any negativity or distortions in your window of perception. You are releasing whatever it is that you need to release in the way of boundaries, tension, and fear. During exhalation, your mind is extending *ki* to the farthest shores of the universe. Although the physical body will have completely exhaled, the mind will be continuously extending out. This complete surrender to the universe through visualization and *ki* extension will allow for a smooth transition between exhalation and inhalation. There is no tension or sudden break in the breathing process. You are becoming one with the universe through expansion or inhalation and one with the universe through complete surrender with each exhalation. Each breath moves in or out from that one infinitely small point of center.

This exercise can be done in any amount of time available, from a couple of minutes to a half hour. Used periodically throughout the day, it will become a powerful tool to rejuvenate and revitalize mind, body, and spirit. The duration of each breath will vary with the individual and will increase through regular practice. The important thing is to connect powerfully and fully with the *ki* of the universe, letting go of boundaries while receiving power, healing, and clarity.

This simple breathing can be done without the polishing movement and in any position, from lying down to riding on a subway.[13] It can be done quietly and discreetly without bothering others. No matter what position you are in, if you are centered first, your body will make the necessary adjustments to effectively do the exercise. Any slouching, limp, or tense position will be changed naturally to one of power and alignment.

Use this exercise daily to release and move any "stuck" energy, and to connect fully with your true purpose and vision and with the world around you. Your health, vitality, and clarity will grow immensely.

# THE ABILITY TO RESPOND

In Aiki workshops, I teach the participants a remarkable *ki* extension exercise that demonstrates the distinction between reacting and responding. I get down on my knees and have a person stand in front of me and place his hands on my shoulders and attempt to push me over. No matter how hard he pushes, even with the assistance of others, his straining and struggling are to no avail. I add to his frustration by continuing to smile and explain what I am doing while he is pushing.

The exercise dramatically demonstrates the principle of connectedness. As he reaches to touch my shoulders, I touch him under the elbows very gently and lightly. By connecting to his energy I can feel the direction and intensity of his pressure. By adding my energy to his, I allow his pressure to literally pass through my shoulders and dissipate into the ground in back of me rather than have it push against my center.

As I teach the workshop participants how to do this exercise, I see their old beliefs about personal power begin to crumble around them. As they easily handle intense pressure applied directly on them by an outside force, they experience the ability to take responsibility for themselves *and* for the energy around them.

When they think they've "got it," I have one of the participants kneel in front of me. I place my hands on his shoulders and gently increase the pressure to make sure that he is centered. I then step back, separating myself from him by several feet, and walk toward him. I touch him with no greater force than before, but immediately upon my contact, the participant topples over, bewildered. He knows I pushed him no harder than before, yet he is no longer able to deal with the situation.

"One of the things we do in life is to wait for things to happen to us, then try to 'get our act together' to handle the new situation," I explain. "Even though we may have all the skills and tools to handle a situation appropriately, we often find ourselves pulling them off the shelf and dusting them off while the truck is already running over us. To be in the world in a manner in which you are merely reacting to it is to be like a leaf in the wind, a victim of circumstances. To respond is a different matter altogether."

I again separate myself from the kneeling participant.

"Do you notice that you have the ability to extend *ki* and touch me right now?" I ask. "In my intention, my hands are already on your shoulder, even though the physical proximity is different. By choice, you can extend *ki* or expand your sphere of influence so that touch has, in effect, already happened. *You* are choosing to touch me. As I begin to walk toward you, I am merely increasing the intensity of the connection that you have already established. As you recall, I will be pushing no harder than I was in the first part of the exercise."

This time when I approach him, his arms naturally come up to meet mine, in perfect timing. Instead of waiting for the pressure of conflict, he is responding effectively and appropriately. My push has no effect.

The ability to extend *ki* is real, and your relationship to the environment around you becomes one of response rather than reaction.

There are no limits to our ability to extend *ki*. When we do so, we naturally expand our personal power and influence on the world around us.

## TAKING RESPONSIBILITY

By extending *ki* or increasing connectedness, we take the most important first step toward the resolution of any conflict because we are creating and nurturing an environment of acceptance, compassion, and trust. It is in this environment that we deeply touch the lives of others.

At the age of thirty, Dr. Albert Schweitzer abruptly left his three doctoral degrees and careers as an author and musician to spend the rest of his life in Africa as a medical missionary. His connection to his fellow human beings extended to all of mankind, and his influence is still powerfully felt today.

———————

Every man has to see in his own way how to make his own self more noble and to realize his own worth. You must give some time to your fellow man. Even if it's a little thing, do something for those who have need of help, something for which you get no pay but the privilege of doing it. For remember, you don't live in a world all your own. Your brothers are here, too.[14]

———————

Reaching out to others is a natural state when you accept your connectedness. Even in her failing health and considerable pain, Eleanor Roosevelt continued to reach out. A few days after she died, a housewife in Tacoma, Washington, received a check for ten dollars. The woman was the daughter of an unemployed hitchhiker whom Mrs. Roosevelt had picked up years before. She found him a job and, gratefully, he promised to name his daughter after the First Lady. After his daughter was born, Mrs. Roosevelt continued to correspond. Every birthday, she would send the girl ten dollars. The last check was signed, feebly but legibly, A. E. Roosevelt. It was mailed the day she died.[15]

When Father Bruce Ritter's theology students challenged him to "practice what he preaches," he left Manhattan College and moved to the Lower East Side of New York to work with the city's poor. Late one winter night in 1968, six homeless kids knocked on his door and asked for a place to sleep. He let them in. The next day, four more arrived.

To Father Ritter, these children were not a problem to be solved. They were unique and fragile human beings with special needs. He accepted them as they were and cared for their immediate needs—food, clothing, shelter—while looking for ways to help them establish meaningful lives.

Responding from his own faith and his commitment to live as it directed him, Father Ritter started a simple and powerful program that provides street kids with the structure and values they need to make real choices about their own lives. The success of his Covenant House program, which in addition now operates in Toronto, Houston, Fort Lauderdale, and New Orleans, is a reflection of his own choice and the ability of his people to connect with the scared, mistrustful children who come searching for help.

Sometimes being able to take responsibility for your life and to powerfully influence those around you is a real test of the principle of connectedness. Try to imagine yourself as a captive, like one of the American hostages in Iran or a POW. Your activities are no longer under your control. You cannot eat when you are hungry, enjoy a walk or take a nap when you feel like it. Your entire life is controlled by someone else.

For most captives, losing control over their daily lives is more frightening than their more widely publicized sufferings—the threats of execution, hunger, beatings, torture, and isolation. One American hostage, upon returning from captivity in Iran, described what was for him the essence of life: "the simple act of brushing my teeth when I get up in the morning, just because I feel like it."

The captives who triumphed managed somehow to reassert command over their destiny. Instead of becoming totally passive and helpless, they used every opportunity they could find to reaffirm their power.

Whenever hostage John Limbert's Iranian guards came into his room, he invited them to sit down. "They became *my* guests," says Limbert, "and in this small way, I established command of the situation. I created the unmistakable sense that this was *my* space, *my* territory, and it did wonders for my well-being."

Early in 1980, when an Algerian delegation made a ceremonial visit, Limbert and a few friends had some candies and fruits left over from their Christmas service. "We made a little plate filled with these goodies," recalls Limbert, "and as the Algerians sat down, we offered the refreshments to them and to the Iranian cameraman who was there to film the occasion for propaganda purposes. The message got through. *We* were the gracious hosts and *they* were our guests. They were visiting at our pleasure, not the other way around." [16]

Eleanor Roosevelt, Schweitzer, Ritter, and Limbert experienced the power of extending *ki*. When we choose to extend *ki*, we have a positive influence on everything around us. We become responsible for our lives, rather than victims.

# TRANSFORMING YOUR FEAR

Fear is a contraction of *ki*. When we close down our energy sphere, we create significant boundaries between our internal thoughts and the external world around us. We react to this separation with an increased feeling of discomfort and anxiety.

One of the most common fears that people have is that of speaking or standing alone in front of a group. In workshops, I use this fear as an excellent opportunity to demonstrate the real power of extending *ki* and of turning fear into power.

Fear is based on getting stuck in time. We are worried about a possible future occurrence, usually based on a past experience (either actual or imagined). When we stand alone in front of a group, our attachment to having the approval of others comes to the surface almost immediately. Fearful that they might discover who we "really" are, with all our human frailties and vulnerabilities, we imagine the group criticizing, snickering, and shaking their heads in disgust. We feel an uncomfortable pressure from all these judging and evaluating stares, pushing us deeper into a tight box of fear and isolation.

The way to handle fear is to step out of our remembrances of the past or fantasies of the future and return to the present moment. This can be done simply by taking deep breaths and returning to center (as discussed in Chapter 4). As you become centered, your awareness will be heightened. Begin to notice what is going on right now within your body. What exactly are you feeling, and where? As your awareness becomes more present, you will begin to experience the "fear" as a physical sensation, such as a tightness in the stomach or a shaking of the legs or a flushed hot sensation in the face and neck. As you breathe deeply from center and become present in the moment, your awareness alone will begin to dissolve the symptoms.

More amazingly, that sense of apprehension will be dissolving as well. You have become present in this moment, and the fear which resides in time (of future expectations based on past experiences) dissipates. This is not to negate the usefulness of the sensation of fear. It can be of value as a tool that informs you of potential harm, but only if you use it as a reminder and cue to become centered and aware, in the present, of what is actually taking place in your body and in your environment. From this centered place, you will deal with each situation more appropriately. Instead of acting out of fear, you will respond with power and clarity of purpose.

When you react to fear by contracting further, you are choosing to close down your energy sphere, to bring it more tightly in on you. Your tendency is to feel that this contraction is being caused by the pressure coming from the outside, rather than to see it's of your own choosing—the contraction is your response to your own self-imposed pressures.

When a workshop participant is in the front of the room, I have him go through the centering and awareness aspects in detail. As he becomes fully present, I ask the question, "Who exactly in the audience is the *most* scary, making you have this fear?" As he begins to actively scan the audience to pick out the culprit, what do you think happens? The person becomes calmer, more present and centered than ever before, because his *ki* is extending, connecting. He is choosing to expand his attention rather than to contract it into a state of judging himself. Suddenly, everything has reversed and an amusing thing happens. Now the audience starts to react with anxiety and discomfort, praying that they won't be picked as the evil one. Now they get to deal with fear. And it is their choice.

As the person in the front of the room extends *ki* and embraces the world, he discovers that no one actually seems scary to him. He has turned his own fear into power, the power to be centered and to powerfully connect with the world around him. The world feels loved in return.

## STOPPING THE FLOW IN MOTOWN

Traveling as John Denver's special assistant was, for me, an unending series of learning experiences in the art of Aiki. It provided a continual opportunity to work on centering and extending *ki*.

When John sings before eighteen thousand people, a very powerful demonstration of connectedness takes place. Each person feels as if John is singing directly to him in the intimate privacy of his own home. When John is centered, his ability to extend *ki* is such that it radiates throughout a large, impersonal arena and yet connects directly to the heart of each person.

One difficulty we encountered was the unique center stage arrangement that John used in large arenas holding ten thousand or more people. When entering one of these arenas, John inevitably had to walk the length of a basketball court down an aisle only two or three feet wide in order to reach the stage. We would do this in complete darkness, to avoid the adoring-fan traffic jam that would inevitably occur if they were aware of his presence.

Exiting after the concert was a more interesting situation. The audience now knew which aisle John would be using, and because the feeling of affection for John at the end of a concert is always high, there was an increased interest in grabbing him, touching him, speaking to him, or stopping him. Letting this go unchecked in a crowd of eighteen thousand people would be uncomfortably close to cannibalism.

What a great opportunity for Aiki training. We chose to walk quickly and quietly down these long aisles without resorting to some sort of heavy-handed police or bodyguard escort. Using Aiki, our technique was to move from center, with *ki* extended strongly, not moving anxiously or too rapidly. We visualized ourselves floating free on a nonstop river to the dressing room, seeing people along the sides as supporting us in getting there, rather than being overly worried about them stopping us. It worked marvelously. During the entire five years I worked with John in concert, we had no problems moving through the aisles.

The one exception, however, came when we tested the system accidentally. We were at Olympia Stadium in Detroit. John had just finished a two-and-a-half-hour concert. Fans, as usual, were giving him a standing ovation. We left the stage together, myself in the lead, extending *ki* through the long exit to the tunnel. As we reached the end of the floor area and were entering the tunnel, John, thinking he was clear of the floor area, stopped to talk to a fan who was above him seated in the stands. As he did so, a woman who must have weighed three hundred pounds reached her large arm over from several rows up in the stands, grabbed John around the shoulders, and lifted him up toward the stands.

All my training in aikido techniques had nothing that spoke to this difficulty. I could not reach her arm to gently press a pressure point, a technique I had used effectively in the past that usually releases the grip. So instead, I was left with the recourse of grabbing John around the legs. I pulled down on his legs; the woman pulled him up, nearly off his feet, by his shoulders.

I could imagine the photo and headline in the paper the next day: SUPERSTAR GROWS FOUR INCHES AFTER HUMAN TUG-OF-WAR. About fifteen seconds of this struggle went on before we got John back to his normal shape, with his feet on the floor.

Stopping the flow of our *ki* in Motown certainly got us "hung up." When you stop the flow of your life, be prepared to swim in the rivers you have created.

# CONNECTING SPIRIT/DISSOLVING EGO

In the summer of 1972, I was practicing the ancient Chinese art of tai chi chuan with Dr. Robert Bishop and tai chi master Marshall Ho'o. We decided to form an international martial arts academy that would bring together under the same roof, for the first time, the martial arts from China, Japan, Korea, the Philippines, and the United States.

We realized that up to that point in time, most of the martial arts in this country had been diluted and stripped of "art" and the public left only with the flashy version presented in the movies and on TV. Our purpose was to bring together the arts in their full context, with the meditative, philosophical, and historical aspects intact. We would gather the foremost practitioners and teachers in a spirit of cooperation and sharing. Thus began the Aspen Academy of Martial Arts, a renowned martial and healing arts institute that flourished over a ten-year period.

In an atmosphere of high expectation we gathered the instructors together. I knew from my corporate business days that organizations of people inevitably have their difficulties, given the wide diversity of personal goals and needs. Little did we know that we were embarking on an in-depth training in international and cultural relations as well. My appreciation for the difficulties people experience in resolving conflict on an international level rose enormously.

I was still naive enough to assume that all Orientals had similar views on life and that any differences we might have would be effortlessly resolved in a calm, traditional Zen-like manner. I experienced quite soon the historical fact that certain Far Eastern nations have rarely gotten along with each other, that we Caucasians are sometimes still considered "barbarians" by some Orientals, and that no matter what their nationality, certain people don't like others very much. Add to that the fact that each individual martial art is notoriously isolated and protective of its own style, and you've suddenly created a great opportunity to learn about conflict.

Can you imagine the first time we met around a table to discuss the logistics of working together? I learned things by the most rapid method known to man—making as many mistakes in as short a time as possible. I started in the classic barbarian mode, asking direct and to-the-point questions such as "OK. How committed are we to this project?" Answers came back in the form of stony silences, stoic demeanors, and circular, indirect, and seemingly irrelevant answers. "It's going to be a long summer," I thought. Of course, we then went out and created one.

All my dreams and expectations of cooperating in a loving, sharing mode gave me my first "whack of the *shinai*," or sudden teaching. It's true that we were all in alignment about the general vision of a martial arts academy based on cooperation and the unique impact and contribution such an organization would have on the martial arts community. But as the organization began to emerge in reality over the first summer, it became more a matter of each instructor trying to get the other instructors enrolled in his own vision of how cooperation should look.

To the extent that we were being "right" about our own art as the correct path, we each felt that cooperation meant that everyone should go along with the way *his* art saw it, or that the logistics of class scheduling and general activities should support *his* art. Each of us was conscientious about setting an example as instructors, and aware that confronting the growing conflict might cause someone else to "lose face," a matter rarely taken lightly in the traditional martial arts. We kept our mouths shut in public and grumbled in private. Each instructor did his own thing. Throughout the day we would have two or three classes going on simultaneously in different areas. We were all so busy doing our own art that we created little time for sharing or even witnessing the others. The only thing we had really accomplished at the academy was to pull isolated arts closer geographically.

It was the students who forced us to look at the hidden conflict and to accept the reality of our connectedness. Since the average student was studying two or three different arts throughout the day, he inevitably found some contradictions. And the more of a beginner he was, the more confusing the differences were. The students requested a day to have us all on a panel to answer questions. There we were, seven of us, being asked disturbingly direct questions. "Which martial art is superior?" "If Mr. Duggan would fight Mr. Kobayashi, who would win?" "One of you says this technique is most effective when you are attacked in this manner, and the other says that this one is. Who is correct?" Another splendid opportunity to swallow our egos and begin to connect. Over the next few hours we found ourselves truly cooperating for the first time.

The lesson that was indelibly learned was that we didn't need to look alike, think alike, or believe alike. We did need to accept our connectedness (in this case, as martial artists and as students of mind and body coordination) and acknowledge all the differences as important contributions to the whole. We discovered that a willingness to accept another's sense of the truth does not invalidate our own, no matter how contradictory it appears. Thanks to the students, that first "confrontation" created within us a connectedness that led quite rapidly to an intensive interest in learning from one another. We instructors began to set aside one day each week to gather and share.

As we let go of our fear of being vulnerable and of not knowing and looking bad, we began to get in touch with the pure enjoyment of exploring, learning, and playing again. The feeling of connectedness and camaraderie increased weekly, as did our individual knowledge and teaching ability. As our team became more trusting and open with each other through daily contact and learning exchanges, the whole academy became a joyful place in which to learn and grow. Being willing to appreciate our differences and to explore our commonality broke loose some of the iron chains of the ego and its confining need always to be right.

## A REPATTERNING EXERCISE

Recall a conflict you've had that did not work out as well as you would have liked. It could be anything from a small breakfast-table squabble to an ongoing, deep-seated dispute that brought forth great animosity.

Relive the experience as vividly as if you were involved in it now. Exactly what did the experience look like, sound like, feel like? What were your facial expressions like? What was your overall physiology and tension level? How would you rate your level of calmness and your tone of voice in the heat of the conflict? How were these facial expressions, sounds, or feelings received by the other person? Did they mitigate the conflict? Did they exacerbate the conflict? Remembering that only a small part of communication is the spoken word, do you feel your overall communication conveyed your best intentions? Was the quality of your communication hindered by your need to be right or to prove the other person wrong?

Did you need to defend your own beliefs or attack someone else's? Did this cause you to operate in the conflict as if the other person was primarily an enemy or opponent? Did the state you were in during the conflict inhibit your ability to notice any potential benefits?

We have the ability to repattern the way we respond to conflict. A powerful process of repatterning is to become centered and then to relive the experience in a harmonious and balanced state.

To do this, we must first recapture the quality of being centered. By breathing deeply, scan your body for points of tension and relax them. Exchange them for flowing energy, naturally expanding outward. See yourself as stable, balanced, and relaxed—a clear vision of fulfillment. Feel a deep sense of aliveness and vitality. To further strengthen the state, you can remember past experiences in your life —times of great success, fulfillment, or happiness—in which you operated in that powerful and peaceful state of centeredness.

As you reexperience the conflict, live and in the present, periodically recenter yourself. See yourself acting in a manner which truly demonstrates your highest intentions. Hear yourself speaking in a sincere and peaceful tone that is supportive of interest and understanding. From this centered state, respond with a heightened sensitivity to and acknowledgment of the other person's good thoughts and highest needs. In this centered state of increased awareness, observe the many unforeseen benefits and opportunities that occur as you relive the conflict. If you sense the other person contracting, or in any way showing fear, anger, or upset, consciously extend your *ki* toward him. This will keep you from contracting, which is a result of getting caught up in your own guilt and/or fear. Make *ki* extension your conscious choice. When we understand that negativity and contraction from another are simply inappropriate ways of crying out for love and support, it is far easier to extend *ki* and exhibit compassion for him.

The mind can be as powerfully retrained by the imagination as it is by reality. The benefits of the repatterning exercise can occur at any time. Do this exercise anytime you "blow it" in a conflict situation and want to imprint deeply a more elegant and appropriate pattern of response. Doing it soon after the event is certainly the most effective way of repatterning an inappropriate response, but even cleaning up a reaction from years ago will be beneficial.

This process requires rolling up your sleeves and working on yourself. Most of us go through life in a hypnotic trance, reacting to others in knee-jerk and unconscious ways. Many of these old patterns do not work very well for either side, yet we've repeated the patterns so often they've become deeply imbedded. As we purpose-fully re-create past experiences in our mind and implant positive patterns or behavior, we begin to take responsibility for the relationships in our lives. Rather than judge ourselves when we find we are operating in a less-than-positive way, it is more beneficial to be grateful and consider the experience as a new learning opportu-nity. Then take a few moments to re-create the more appropriate responses. Remember that if we react inappropriately in a conflict, it is not too late to work on repatterning. It can be done as powerfully before or after the real event. Drop by drop, day by day, we can transform ourselves and our relationships. Life becomes a fertile ground for learning and growing.

## Risk Takers

• When you find yourself at a tollbooth, pay the attendant for the car behind you also. Just drive on as if nothing unusual had happened. If the car following drives alongside yours in an at-tempt to figure you out, expand your *ki* sphere with a smile or a nod, as if to say "Have a nice day" or "I just enjoy feeling con-nected."

• If you are in a grocery store and you find yourself feeling down and separate from the world, get centered, extend *ki*. Have that shopping cart become part of you and an extension of your arms. You'll find yourself walking centered, extended, down the aisles and things will immediately appear more connected, more fun, more of an experience. Everything's new again. Even the Muzak is inspirational. Extending *ki* and moving from center may be applied in any situation, no matter how mundane. It repatterns any negative thoughts from the past, takes the boredom out of the task, and replaces it with a sense of mystery and discovery.

• When you find yourself riding in a car or on a bicycle, or walking, establish eye contact with people that you don't know. Smile and wave at them. Recall what it feels like when someone spontaneously waves or says hi to you. Then share that feeling with others. You don't need to know a person to communicate a sense of connection.

● Try out this Buddhist meditation technique as you go through your day. Focus your love and energy on someone and use your breathing as a technique to relieve his "pain." By inhaling, you are taking his pain away. By exhaling, you are releasing it and freeing him. This lovely gift of connecting can be done for anyone familiar or unfamiliar, close at hand or far away.

● When you're in a public place, such as a park or beach, or even a city street, pick up that can or paper bag that you see lying there. It will make a difference, and if you routinely do so, it could have a positive influence on those around you, suggesting that they too are part of the mess *and* the solution.

---

### THE AIKI APPROACH

#### Accept Your Connectedness

Connectedness *is* reality. Separation is an illusion.

*Ki,* or energy, is the thread which connects all things. *Ki* is verifiable, measurable, and without limits.

Relationship is all about contraction and expansion. We can choose to expand our *ki* and strengthen our connection, or to contract our *ki* and increase our feeling of separateness.

True strength is flowing energy and a willingness to blend energies.

Unlimited strength and power are available to the extent that we let go of tension, fear, and boundaries.

*In every real man a child is hidden that wants to play.*
Friedrich Nietzsche

# 6. The Power of Discovery

Mark Twain once summed up his life. "I became a silver-miner in Nevada; next, a newspaper reporter; next, a gold-miner; next, a special correspondent in the Sandwich Islands; next, a roving correspondent in Europe and the East; next, an instructional torchbearer on the lecture circuit; and, finally, I became a scribbler of books, and an immovable fixture among the other rocks of New England." [17]

The domain of discovery is a magical one. It allows us to move beyond the fight, beyond success, to an open realm of possibility.

Look at the masters of discovery—infants. There is no evaluation when an infant is learning. There is no good, bad, right, or wrong. It is all discovery. When an infant successfully grasps an object in her crib for the first time or stands upright and walks, she doesn't need to look around for approval. She is too busy discovering. When she knocks over a glass of milk, she doesn't feel guilty. She's too busy examining the flow, the texture, and the interesting patterns the milk makes on the tablecloth. She *is* discovery.

Discovery is moving naturally and appropriately in the universe. As for conflict, you are not stuck on any position, but are willing to explore, to be aware of what is, and to look for all possibilities of what can be.

Discovery is the power of opening yourself up to all that the universe has to offer.

When Master Ueshiba was just a young student of the martial arts, his travels brought him to an inn, where he met the legendary Sokaku, the founder of the Daito-ryu school of aiki-jutsu and master teacher to literally tens of thousands of students. Ueshiba was just brash enough in his youth to challenge the master to a test of their fighting skills. He proved no match for Master Sokaku. Instead of going home humiliated with his tail between his legs or in rage at his defeat, Ueshiba got down on his knees and bowed to Sokaku with respect and gratitude. His need to discover was greater than his need to win. For the next month he remained with Sokaku, immersed in every word and movement. All this time, Ueshiba's family and friends back home thought he had perished in a blizzard. But Ueshiba's discovering attitude left him enraptured in study. Upon his return home, he built a *dojo* (a martial arts practice area) and invited Sokaku to live there. Years later Ueshiba said, "Those who seek to study Aikido should open their minds. . . . We go forward in life with this attraction of our spirit and attempt to command a whole view of the world." [18]

# DISCOVERY WITH A MASTER

*The little I know, I owe to my ignorance.*
    Sacha Guitry
    *Toutes Reflexions Faites*

A few years ago I was with John Denver and a group of researchers in Hawaii filming the humpback whales. I thought our purpose was to create a TV special, but fortunately I was mistaken. I was there to learn the principle of discovery.

Being with these great creatures of the deep is a close encounter of another kind. As adults, humpbacks are thirty to fifty feet long and weigh thirty to fifty tons. They have a cerebral cortex as convoluted and as complex as ours, and much larger. It has been estimated that we have been around about fifty thousand years in our present state of brain development. They've been around, in their present state, about thirty million years. Yet they fall far short of humans in their ability to manipulate their universe. Unlike humans, they don't have the manipulators, the thumbs. Isn't that phenomenal? Who are these beings who have been around that long, with that big a brain, who haven't had to rape, pillage, and plunder their environment to survive? Is it possible that humans could learn something from these great beings of the oceans who have been evolving on this planet for many millions of years longer than we have?

John was in the water with a mother, a nurse (a large male who accompanies a mother and baby) and a calf, about a hundred yards away from the boat. There was one person in the water with him, filming. I was with the dive crew waiting on the boat to do whatever was needed, when Roger Payne, the resident whale-expert, noticed the mother vigorously waving her head in the water, turning the quiet seas into surfable water. Roger thought she might be signaling alarm or warning because John had gotten between her and the calf. And a slap of her tail—a mother's slap, if you will—is not something you would want to feel. Roger waved John back to the boat. To make certain that John received the message, researcher Dan McSweeney and I swam out in scuba gear. Visibility was only about sixty feet. John had understood the first signal, however, and had started back to the boat, passing us unnoticed.

As Dan and I were swimming out, thinking John was still with the whales, we saw a huge shadow suddenly appearing, like a Mack truck on a dark, foggy night. Whales can accelerate up to thirty-five knots in very little time. At fifty tons, that's *real* fast. With that visibility and that speed, by the time we could clearly see the whale it would be past us—or worse, through us. Even knowing all the stories about what wonderful, benign creatures whales are, all our *Jaws* memories came right back. Here was this incredible shadow coming at us at full speed. We were paralyzed with fear, and hung in the water, holding hands, thinking "I guess this is it!" At the last moment, the whale miraculously made a sharp, banking turn and stopped on a dime, with a huge eye, not ten feet away, staring right through us.

There we were, Dan and I. The terror we had felt was somehow transformed into an indescribable peace. It was like being in the presence of a Master. The lesson that took place in that moment was inscribed forever deeply into my being: *I don't know anything.* I felt my insignificance on a level I had never experienced before. I gave up everything I knew, involuntarily. I didn't consciously give it up, *it was given up.*

At the moment I let go, there was an incredible peace. The lesson was clear to me—giving up my significance, giving up what I knew, put me in a place of discovery that was unbelievably powerful.

The whale hovered there for about thirty seconds, but it seemed like an eternity. Eventually it dropped down ten feet and to our astonishment made some sounds and another whale appeared. We hadn't known the big male was there, but it became apparent that this large whale had swum up to us totally synchronized with the mother, the two like two great spaceships in the night. After the whales spoke briefly in an eerie repertoire of strange gurgles and beeps, they did a great, banking turn past us, perfectly synchronized. As they did, we saw the calf riding a foot above the mother. We had been so caught up in her presence that we hadn't realized there were three whales until they started moving away and we were back to normal consciousness. The three of them had come like three great ships, stopped on a dime in front of us for an eternity, communicated with each other (probably about the eccentric behavior of this strange new species on the planet, homo sapiens), and swum off, leaving whale skin all over Dan as they gently brushed past him.

There are fresh and new perspectives to everything in life if we let go of the filters of our past and the blinders of our expectations. To be able to embrace all of life as an opportunity to discover brings forth magic, growth, and aliveness.

# BELIEVING VERSUS DISCOVERY

*Nothing is more dangerous than an idea when it is the only one you have.*
                                                    Emile Chartier

Rigid belief systems are the root of violence.[19] I define a rigid belief system as a structure or mind-set to which you are attached. You can tell that you have a belief system if you find yourself continuously defending it. Belief systems create boundaries. There are, by definition, things inside those boundaries and things outside. In other words, when you create a set of anything, you have excluded everything else. If you have a set of golf clubs, you tend to make sure that hockey sticks stay out of it. If you have a belief that bosses never listen to their employees, you will refrain from initiating honest, effective communication with your boss when it is most needed.

In a rigid belief system, anything that jeopardizes those boundaries must be defended against. One way to fulfill this constant need for defense is to attack other belief systems before they attack you. Belief systems are often a catalyst for violence. How many wars can we count that have been fought over religious beliefs? The greater the differences between the beliefs and the stronger the fervor of the beliefs, the greater the violence. Much of the violence we experience daily, however, is going on internally. We are at war within, constantly defending our old beliefs from new and opposing beliefs and thoughts (even if these new thoughts are of our own making). We begin to witness where the root of all violence lives—within ourselves and our need to protect our belief systems.

Discovery is different. When you discover something you don't need to defend it or attack others' ideas about it. Let's say you have an apple in your hand. When the apple is released from your grasp, you notice that it goes down. Every time. Not up, but down. You begin to perceive that apples go down. You don't have a need to convince yourself or others about your experience. Let's suppose a friend or foe came rushing in one day claiming, "Guess what? Apples go up when I drop them." Imagine your reaction. You wouldn't angrily defend your own perception about apples or attack him viciously for such heretical thoughts. You would most likely have a great interest in and fascination with his experience.

Discovery is a mind-set in which you are naturally open to having your beliefs changed radically, or even having them disappear all together. You have no attachment to what you truly know. If your perception changes through another experience, fine. It is only belief systems that need to be protected. Belief systems take energy to constantly protect their boundaries. There are always potential "enemies" to your belief systems for whom you must be on the alert. To deal with violence effectively in the world, we need to begin to let go of that violent place inside of ourselves, of the need to defend territory, make judgments, and attack others.

How do you change the violent nature of belief systems into a more discovering and open system of perceptions? By simply being aware of them. If you *try* to rid yourself of belief systems, declaring how bad they are and beating yourself up for having them, you've only created another belief system. You are setting yourself up for just another battle, taking time and energy from where it is truly needed—in discovering what is actually there and dancing appropriately with it.

If you are walking down a street and a car turns into your path, you naturally and quickly move out of the way. It does not require a belief that moving cars are evil to have an appropriate response. You only need awareness, not beliefs, to dance appropriately and successfully in life.

The need to judge absolutely or to become self-righteous about our opinions will eventually do violence to ourselves. Maintaining a clear awareness of the stressful and injurious nature of judging and self-righteous mind-sets is the most important step in naturally discontinuing this activity. The harm comes not from *having* opinions, but from the awareness and freedom we lose by casting them in concrete.

Heightening our awareness is the most effective tool we can use in dealing with any addiction to injurious habits. For example, if we are interested in giving up overeating, we can heighten our awareness of exactly what it is that we are doing to ourselves at all levels, from social to cellular.

It is a common tendency for us to misinterpret spiritual or relationship hunger for physical hunger. When we are "unconscious" of the distinction, we move like robots to the refrigerator every time we feel a lack of something. This unconscious patterning finds us reacting to feelings of loneliness, unworthiness, or anger in a self-defeating fashion—gulping and swallowing our way to an even greater hunger for self-esteem and fulfillment.

As we heighten our awareness, our perceptions take on an increased lucidity and fascination and our choices become clearer and more spontaneously correct. As you take the time to see what exactly is on your plate, to listen to and taste each bite through careful chewing, to get in touch with your feelings and energy level as a result, you will take a major step in choosing the right foods for you.

When you are physically hungry, you naturally eat food slowly, consciously, and appreciatively. When you are emotionally hungry, you naturally fill your plate with friends, hugs, and good thoughts, all prepared with forgiveness and love. Increasing our awareness will provide us with a more complete menu from which to fill our needs. As we change the game from one of judgment based on beliefs to one of discovery, we naturally begin to let go of those mind-sets that do not work in our lives. Our ability to move more freely and without limits takes a quantum leap forward.

*Loyalty to a petrified opinion never yet broke a chain or freed a human soul.*
Mark Twain

# A CURE FOR HAVING TO BE "PERFECT"

The power of discovery enables us to achieve excellence without having to be "perfect."

Most of us are, in one form or another, perfectionists. For us to feel good about ourselves, we must be perfect. Being perfect is based on a particular performance level. And our performance levels are usually derived from role models or scores against opponents. If we are playing golf, perfection is matching Jack Nicklaus or, at the very least, shooting par. If we're in the office, being perfect may mean beating out all the competition for top salesman of the year.

We become so goal- or destination-oriented that we get stuck, afraid of not reaching our future expectations or of repeating a past mistake. With the fear of failure firmly entrenched, we become unwilling to take risks. Yet it's the willingness to take risks, to explore our limits, that is key to achieving excellence and reaching our full potential. However, we, the perfectionists, see only a right and a wrong way to do something. And if we fail in our desired result, we are not perfect and therefore not OK. When our self-esteem is threatened, we naturally resort to defending ourselves or attacking others to insure the survival of our ego. Excess energy is spent on judgment, fear, and frustration.

Instead of breaking our golf clubs around a tree, how can we, the perfectionists, turn our life of frustration into an art of fascination? The secret is in the power of discovery.

When we are willing to be wrong, we increase our willingness to risk or to explore the outer limits of our potential. The discovery attitude increases our awareness and acceptance of, and attention to, what is. We are fully present in the process and willing to do whatever it takes.

Henry Ford had already gone bankrupt twice and was still willing to risk everything to develop the "horseless carriage." Walt Disney went bankrupt five times in pursuit of his fantasy world of joy and discovery, Disneyland. And Richard Bach was turned down fifty-three times before one publisher "discovered" his talent and published *Jonathan Livingston Seagull*.

Let's look at a specific example. Joe Baggodonuts' boss asks him to do a financial feasibility study of a project. Joe does the report and it shows that, financially, the project won't work. The next week Joe just happens to overhear the boss slam the report down on his desk and exclaim, "I don't like this one bit!"

If Joe draws only on his past knowledge and fears, he may think, *Uh oh. I know the boss doesn't like me. He doesn't like the way I did that report. I know he thinks I'm incompetent. Well, come to think of it, I don't like him very much either. You know what I don't like about him? Talk about incompetence. Why, just the other day . . .*

What Joe thinks he knows escalates into a reaction. He perceives his ego as threatened, and he needs to defend himself or attack his boss to keep his self-esteem intact.

If Joe were open to discovery, he would be aware of what is and not be the prisoner of assumptions. Joe could let go of all his preconceived ideas, opinions, and judgments. Instead of assuming that the boss thinks his report was wrong and therefore his competence is lacking, Joe could diplomatically ask about the boss's thoughts, going directly to the source—the boss—and avoiding the coffee shop–gossip syndrome. He may discover, much to his amazement, that the boss considers his report excellently prepared, accurate, and conclusive. What the boss is upset about is not having enough money to do the project.

How many times have you suffered over an incident in a relationship, feeling as if you had "failed" miserably and your entire self-esteem was in jeopardy? Then, days or weeks later, you risk sitting down with your partner to communicate openly about his or her perspective of the same event. And *voilà,* you discover that you had spent all that time tormenting yourself with something you only imagined your partner was perceiving, which couldn't be further from the truth.

The power of discovery encourages us to explore solutions rather than spend excess energy on blame and justification. The energy saved is now used to create and develop projects and ideas that work and, just as important, to have fun and to grow in the process.

Have you ever let your fear of failure keep you from taking a class or joining in an activity you'd like to try? I observed an aerobics dance-class where there was only one male in a large class of women. But instead of hiding uncomfortably in the back row, this guy was going all out in the very middle, not necessarily doing the exercises perfectly or staying with the beat. It was clear to everybody that he was there to exercise and to learn about himself in the process. This attitude of discovery was a gift to the class and the instructor, as well as to himself. It's a secret to moving into a realm beyond success.

*Normally, we do not so much look at things as overlook them.*
Alan Watts

## JUDGING VERSUS DISCOVERY

In organizations from sports teams to big businesses, constructive criticism is regarded as useful and is most often used when things aren't going well. But if the discovery principle is lacking, criticism is often greatly misused. The more a manager or employer or coach gives high priority to criticism, the more he focuses on the past and on what is wrong in the organization, rather than on what is needed. The tendency to constantly evaluate the world around him has become a patterned response. As this tendency grows stronger, criticism, no matter how honest and truthful, inevitably falls short of its good intentions. Conflicts seem to emerge from everywhere.

In a study done in Iowa, graduate students followed a normal two-year-old throughout a day. They observed that the child was told what not to do 432 times, as opposed to 32 positive acknowledgments. The national average of parent-to-child criticisms is 12 to 1—that is, 12 criticisms to 1 compliment. Within the average secondary school classroom, the ratio of criticism to compliments is 18 to 1 between teacher and student.[21] And we wonder why our children so often have low self-esteem?

| THE LIMITS OF PERFECTION | THE POWER OF DISCOVERY [20] |
|---|---|
| Perfection and self-esteem based on doing it a certain way | Discovery and self-esteem based on inquiry and creativity |
| Based on being right | No right or wrong |
| Failure—bad or wrong; fear of failure | Failure—opportunity for greater experience and awareness |
| An unwillingness to take risks | A willingness to take risks, to do whatever it takes |
| Frustration and anxiety | Fascination and enjoyment |
| Control | Spontaneity |
| Judgment of self and others | Appreciation of self and others |
| Work and struggle | Play |

Instead of overly criticizing, let's see how the natural desire to support others can be more effective by applying the principle of discovery.

In criticism, the language that we use often takes on a damaging, judgmental twist. We begin to use the word *you* instead of *I*. Consider these criticisms as if you were on the receiving end:

- You are always late.
- You didn't fix this machine properly.
- Your letter is no good.
- You're out of position again. When are you going to learn to play baseball correctly?

How does the "you" approach feel? Not so good? Do you have the feeling of being judged? Do you feel that your actions are being evaluated as wrong or bad?

When we communicate from a place of discovery, we naturally use "I" or "we." This involves more awareness of other people's needs and feelings, and of our own, and we become more specific as to our desired results. Consider the different ways of communicating:

- You are always late.    *versus*    When I don't have to wait, I feel that the value of my time is acknowledged.

The judging aspect of "you" gets magnified when we add "always." Conflict and resistance are created because it is obviously a gross generalization. Are you *always* late? Were you born late? Will you die late?

- You didn't fix this    *versus*    I can't get this machine to do machine correctly.    what I'd like. I'd like it to . . .

The first statement lays blame, while the second declares your present perception of *your* difficulty. In addition, the second statement communicates specifically the outcome you want.

- Your letter is no good.     *versus*     I'd like your help in getting this
                                            letter to say what I want to
                                            communicate. I need to
                                            communicate the
                                            following: . . .

The first statement again judges and criticizes. It leaves no openings to resolve the conflict. The second statement supports process, learning, and growth.

- You're out of position      *versus*     When we all play our
  again. When are you                      positions, the field is better
  going to learn to play                   covered and we're likely to
  baseball correctly?                      get more outs. It feels great
                                           when we play together as a
                                           team.

Have you ever had a coach who consistently used statements like the first one? The implication is that you are a failure and have *never* been successful and probably never will be. The second communication implies that you have the necessary ability now and also states the reasons behind the coach's desired outcome and the feeling associated with it.

The statements of course can be changed in many ways. Far more important than the specific words used are the attitude and context. If a person is centered, if there is a feeling of rapport and connectedness, and if he or she has a playful, discovering attitude, the essence of his or her communication has taken place even before the words are heard. We feel trusted, respected, and acknowledged.

When a person operates in the present, from discovery, his responses become proactive rather than reactive. He expresses his needs from a responsible *I* viewpoint, rather than telling you what *you* should do. As I said in an earlier chapter, people are generally tired of getting "should on" in their lives, and the "you should" approach creates unnecessary resistance.

## ABOUT BUCKY AND DISCOVERY

Buckminster Fuller[22] is known by most of the world for his superb technological inventions and his clear insights into the working principles of the universe. But for me and many others who knew him personally, he was a grandfather of the fondest kind—one who loved unconditionally and whose twinkle of the eye and compassionate heart made us feel as if we were five years old, sitting wide-eyed on Granddaddy's lap, waiting for the next story.

Bucky was open to discovery. It was one of the consistent things about his personality that moved me. He came across not only as a unique and wise person, but as one who had kept up an innocent, childlike openness to discovery. When he was in school, the teacher would put a line on the board. Bucky would raise his hand and ask, "How much does that weigh?" The teacher's immediate reaction would be, "What a stupid little kid. Can't you see we're talking about geometry? We're talking about lines and dots." He rarely got an answer. Yet somehow he had the tenacity to keep asking questions. That was a good indication that he had an unswerving ability to keep seeking. He was still asking questions at eighty-seven years of age.

Whenever Bucky saw a child, he was drawn like a magnet to play and to discover. With the help of his little black bag—which resembled a doctor's—stuffed full of colorful tubes, hubs, and connectors, Bucky could transform himself into a geometrical magic act, mesmerizing those of all ages. "Children really want to talk about the universe in a big way," explained Bucky. "Things are changing, dear fellow. There's a beautiful evolution going on. Mankind is just continually surprised."

Always permeating his expansive and brilliant mind was the infantlike joy of seeing things new and fresh each day. His eyes were perpetually moist with awe and gratitude at the workings of God in everything around him.

Bucky would get so enraptured by some idea or project that he would frequently stay up all night working at a dining room table, only to be startled when breakfast was suddenly under way all around him. On one such occasion he remarked, "Wow. I do get lost in concentration. When I'm really working, I don't know where I am in the Universe."[23]

He did not separate technology from nature and recognized the divine in all of creation. Bucky blended his absolute trust in the Universe with the guts to stick his neck out for the common good.

We get a sense of Bucky's attitude from his reply to a reporter's question about his love for sailing even in the worst weather. "When I was a child, I was told, 'You can't go out today, it's too rough.' But I always had the feeling that the best things would happen to you only if you did go out."[24]

Each year, Bucky would come to Windstar as a member of our advisory board and to conduct a lecture/workshop for the general public. Just listening to Bucky lecture could itself be a lesson in discovery. Picture a little, bald man with thick glasses, in his mideighties, standing 5'2" tall, in a three-piece suit, walking with a cane. The feeling that an uninformed person would get as Bucky approached the platform was that this man would probably need a rest after thirty or forty minutes and should definitely be watched carefully because activity might be damaging to his health. Hours, and I mean *hours* later (the only thing that could adequately curtail Bucky was the janitor locking doors and turning off lights), the observer would be on the edge of his seat, truly fascinated by the incredible intelligence, passion, and commitment of this one human being.

Although Bucky's language resembled the English language, listening to it word by word would reveal that it was in a totally unique form. When Bucky was a young man he recognized the need to let go of some of his belief systems, to free himself of the hypnotic trance of the culture, and to establish a fresh look. He spent two years in silence in an apartment in Chicago for the purpose of discerning what *he* thought and uncovering the power of language. Upon reentering the speaking world, he noticed he was unable to use words that for him were not in alignment with the basic principles of the universe. For instance, he discovered that there is no "up" or "down" in the universe, only "in," "out" and "around." Therefore, to use "up" or "down" was inappropriate communication. The sun did not rise or set, the earth turned. As Bucky became more and more disciplined about the use of language, he began to speak in an extraordinary new way, assembling words that conveyed, as closely as possible, his own integrity. Even within a language for which there are clear rules, dictionaries, and a history of proper usage, Bucky was willing to let go of what was known and to seek what was most appropriate, honest, and elegant for him.

A first-time listener to Bucky would be struck by his long, run-on sentences, which would lead one to new and different concepts. These concepts would stretch the listener's mind to the point where his memory of all the things Bucky had said since first starting the sentence would lapse.

A typical example:

------

World Game's now clearly demonstrated capability to produce the higher-than-ever-before-experienced living standard means an ever-healthier, ever-less-environmentally-restrained, ever-better-informed and -comprehensively-educated, ever-more-thoughtfully, -spontaneously, and -cooperatively-productive total humanity operating as an ever-more-mutually-intertrusting and -interconsiderate world family, living in an ever-more-generous and less wasteful way, at an ever-more-foresighted and -comprehensively-anticipatory level; engaged in ever-more-constructive initiative-taking and cooperative intersupport of one another's initiatives and explorations; an ever-more-truly omniloving, classless, raceless, human family of Earth's planetarians—all engaged competently in local Universe information-harvesting and in local Universe problem-solving, in successful support of the 100-percent integrity of eternally regenerative Universe, that being the function in Universe that World Game assumes occasioned the inclusion of humans and their generalized-principles-discovering-minds in the design of Universe.[25]

------

I soon learned that it was exceedingly difficult to be constantly debating and fitting what Bucky had to say into cerebral cortex categories. The only way to truly hear Bucky was to let go of what you thought you knew. If you were open to listening, he would somehow amazingly tie it all back together for you. For me, it was not so much the words he spoke that conveyed the essence of his communication, but his compassion and commitment, the inspirational model that he presented for all.

We learned to be prepared for anything when Bucky came to town. When Bucky came to Windstar, he would inevitably discover some new idea that he wanted to test, and he would send us scurrying around to collect the necessary resources. On one particularly memorable occasion, Bucky had been working on a unique geodesic structure, which he lovingly termed a four-frequency deresonated tensegrity structure. He and one of his staff members, Amy Edmondson, had been working on the mathematics of such a structure, but to date, none had been erected. The night before his workshop was to begin, Bucky was to give a Windstar public lecture at the Aspen Institute of Humanistic Studies.

That night, I found myself listening to Bucky at approximately 10 P.M., two thirds of the way through his presentation. To my surprise, he explained, "In tomorrow's workshop we will, for the first time, build a thirty-five-foot-diameter, four-frequency deresonated tensegrity structure. It will be the first one of its kind ever built and an exciting experiment for all."

As I looked over at the Windstar staff members, I saw jaws hanging open. They were thinking, as I was, about how we were going to procure all the necessary wood, nails, and equipment by nine o'clock the next morning.

Immediately following the presentation, I gathered the staff together with pen and pencil in hand and went immediately to Bucky to inquire about what was needed. Bucky ran through the list he had in mind, and after taking two pages of detailed and copious notes, we realized we had quite a job to do. The staff worked late into the night. With pencil and pad in hand, Bucky returned to his own room to spend the rest of the night, except for a couple of hours, at his desk planning for the project. How many of us, in one day, could have flown from the East Coast to the Rocky Mountains, worked a full afternoon at Windstar, given a three- to four-hour lecture, and still been able to stay up all night, wide-eyed and alert, preparing a risky experiment for a workshop that was to begin in the early morning? And all this at the age of eighty-five. Even more amazing, this was not a unique day in Bucky's life but a relatively normal one.

It's one thing to attempt a project in which you are putting yourself on the line. It's another thing, however, to stop a project when the momentum and expectations are high and everyone has committed time and energy beyond the normal call of duty. Our tendency is to disregard evidence that continuing the project no longer meets our purpose. We find it difficult to radically change our original intentions, even though, out of integrity, we must do so. This became very clear when I appeared in my office at Windstar at seven o'clock the next morning, ready to check on all the logistics of the project. Bucky was there and declared immediately, "I have discovered that it was inappropriate to go ahead with the structure at this time. I was not thinking clearly last night and have recognized my errors in calculation."

Upon my desk I found a letter in Bucky's handwriting, entitled boldly "ERRORS." In detail and at length, it enumerated the errors he had made, the discovery of which made continuation of the project infeasible. At the end, written in decidedly larger and clearer letters, were these words:

---

When you have made an error, the first thing to do is to say so quickly and stop the derivative action. STOP!

---

Being open to discover new alternatives and new ideas is important, but it is also essential to maintain that attitude when your mistakes or your inappropriate actions are revealed. It takes real courage to discover your own errors and do something about them without procrastinating or fearing the judgment of others.

*Toto, I don't think we're in Kansas anymore.*
Dorothy
*The Wizard of Oz*

## Risk Takers

• Every once in a while when you have a day which is not too hectic, set it up as a silent day. Obtain the support and permission of people around you beforehand. They can participate or not. As you go through an entire day of silence, it will be such an intense learning experience that it will have far-reaching benefits for everything you do. As you go through several silent days, you will notice that there are different phases of being silent. At first you are silent verbally, but find yourself mentally talking to yourself all day, occasionally even talking out loud and only realizing it afterward. In subsequent silent days you will find yourself more and more aware of the many levels of silence. You will give up the subtle levels of talking to yourself for the far more rewarding feeling of just being in the present and truly listening.

Silent days are a wonderful way for a group to explore and experiment with communication. You may discover that your communication can happen on an even more powerful level. Significant and important needs get taken care of ever more quickly and the idle chatter falls away.

*When real silence is dared, we can come very close to ourselves and to the deep center of the world.*

James Carroll

• Explore your ability to communicate with other species. We may be the only species on the planet to suffer so deeply from interspecies deprivation. Notice how animals respond to you when you give them your undivided attention. Next time you go on a picnic, put aside some of your food for the ants. Actually invite them to your picnic. See what happens. Or carry dog biscuits in your pockets. Animals always live in the present. In spending some conscious time with them, you will discover more about the present yourself.

• Try putting food coloring (or Jello) in your bathtub. Just for the fun of it.

• When you are doing one of those seemingly monotonous chores like washing dishes or mowing the lawn or vacuuming the carpet, become more aware of the present by scrutinizing details, colors, textures, and your movement patterns. Infants do this all the time. Have your *ki* flow from you to the item touched or to the job being done.

● When you're in a relationship, occasionally close your eyes when looking at your friend. As you reopen them, see him or her as totally new, as if you'd never seen him or her before. See colors, textures, sounds, patterns, and feelings, and let go of your past pictures. Notice as many little things as possible: scrutinize your friend as if you're seeing a flower for the first time.

● Pick a subject—such as art, music, dance—in which you feel deficient or inept. Take a few hours by yourself to experiment and create in that art, using the process of discovery to help you supercede the restraints of perfectionism.

*Life is either a daring adventure or nothing.*
Helen Keller

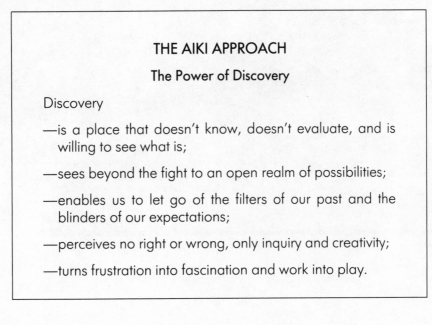

## THE AIKI APPROACH

### The Power of Discovery

Discovery

—is a place that doesn't know, doesn't evaluate, and is willing to see what is;

—sees beyond the fight to an open realm of possibilities;

—enables us to let go of the filters of our past and the blinders of our expectations;

—perceives no right or wrong, only inquiry and creativity;

—turns frustration into fascination and work into play.

# 7. Be Willing to Understand

*Can a blue man sing the whites?*
Algis Juodikis

The world has gotten very noisy. The erratic whine and roar of construction; the constant rumble and shrill horns of traffic; the endless din of radios, TVs, and tape decks—these bang at our eardrums all day long. It's no wonder that under this blitzkrieg against our senses, we often stop listening to nature, to ourselves, and to each other. Even in prayer, which should be a blessed communication with the divine, we neglect the most valuable aspect of the prayerful process —listening. We fold our hands and become like terrorists, making anxious demands on God to meet on our terms and in our time frame. "Ask and you shall receive" becomes "Whine incessantly and you might get it," or "Demand and take what you want."

Those long, quiet nights of the past, with humans sitting around fires or candlelight; the natural rhythms that come from the daily working of the soil and the harvesting of food, or from sitting by a flowing stream—these have drifted into memory. Man now awakens to an unsettling alarm, immediately switches on the TV news and tunes in to the noisy chatter of his already preoccupied mind. Even though we are scientifically aware that our health requires us to understand the world around us and to be understood by it, we neglect the beautiful gift of attentive listening.

To let go of our old images, of the way we think people are, and to see and hear and touch them anew, like a precious being or flower that we've come across for the first time—this is the joy we get from listening. We all know how empowering it is to have a person truly listen to us, without judgment or answers, as an interested and attentive partner, a true friend. Let us explore the power and blessings that result when we are able to give this gift freely in our daily lives and receive its rewards.

## THE APPRECIATION EXERCISE

This exercise will demonstrate to you experientially the difference that being willing to understand can make. Have a partner (let's call him the attacker) reach out and grab your wrist with both of his hands (photograph A). Notice how easy it is for you to get caught up in the attack. Your mind gets caught on the wrist, on the issue. The tendency will be to struggle to move your wrist somehow. In other words, you get caught up exactly where the attacker wants you to be. As long as you stay in your own position and the attacker stays in his, the fight can go on and on.

You do, however, have another choice. You can move off your position—that is, leave the wrist alone and pivot your centered body, as if it were a large ball of energy, along the attacker's arm (photograph B). You now stand side by side with the attacker. From this position, you are out of the way of the direction of the attack and in an excellent position to use the attacker's energy. In nonphysical terms, you have established a commonality of vision and direction, and are therefore in an optimum position to resolve the conflict.

A good way to practice this physical movement is to add a verbal attack to it. Have the attacker say something like "You sure are stupid," or "I'm sick and tired of you always . . . ," or "I don't think you're right. I think . . ." As you move off the line of the attack and join shoulder-to-shoulder with the attacker, you reply, "I appreciate your communication," "I understand," "I see," "I hear," or "I'm interested to learn why you think so," or something to indicate acknowledgment and willingness to understand the other person. A

A                                         B

simple "Yes!" proclaimed strongly and with all your energy behind it will do wonders for integrating your thoughts and emotions with the movement. Acknowledgment alone is often enough to remove the anger and negativity from an attacker's position.

It is very important to know that this does not mean acquiescing to the attacker or admitting that you are wrong and he is right. It instead means a strong and courageous willingness on your part to accept his energy as potentially useful and worthy of your understanding. It is very difficult to apply the old Indian adage, "Do not judge another until you have walked a mile in his moccasins," unless you get out of your own moccasins first.

This exercise can take on a high quality of subtleness and truly test your ability to be centered. If held correctly, a person can only pivot or whirl into alignment alongside an attacker if he himself is truly centered. He must function as one unit or sphere of energy. If he is tense (exhibiting a fighting mind) or limp (weak and fearful) it is very difficult to complete the movement correctly. You learn in a very real way that the Aiki Approach is neither acquiescing nor accommodating out of fear.

In the photo sequence below, aikido uses the appreciation or acknowledgment principle effectively in responding to a physical attack. Rather than struggling, trying to free your wrist through physical manipulation or force, you can use aikido to honor the attack as a gift of energy, move out of the way of the force, and become part of its source. By doing this you can combine your energy with the attacker's to preserve and nurture life rather than harm it.

135

Let's break this complicated-looking "dance" down into a simple "energy geometry" of attack and response.[26] Look at the first photograph again. The attacker is grabbing my wrist with both hands. Notice how his shoulders and arms form a triangle.

The triangle conveys the idea of action aimed in a specific direction. It conjures up images of focused energy. When teaching the martial art aspect of conflict, I have found this triangular form useful for representing attacks—both physical attacks, such as punching, kicking, and grabbing, and mental or emotional attacks in our daily life.

Let's use a circle to represent flowing, rolling, blending responses, such as negotiation, collaboration, acceptance, or "going with the flow."

A square, with its lessened ability to move, can represent the response of holding fast to a position. This may take the form of doing nothing (passive disengagement) in a conflict, or of conscious resistance.

Now let's look at some conflicts from this geometric standpoint.

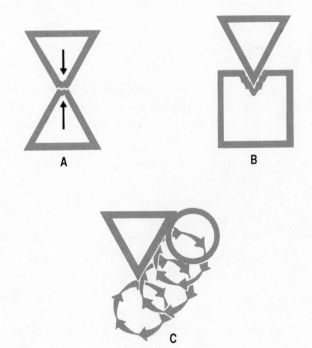

If you respond to an attack by taking on the geometry of a triangle, as in diagram A, you are matching force against force. If you take on the geometry of a square, as in diagram B, you create resistance and lessen your ability to move, as well as increase the possibility of your being "pierced." Taking on the geometry of a sphere or circle, however, results in ease of movement and the ability to create alignment. As we see in diagram C, a sphere can roll and turn naturally. As you can see in the aikido sequence, I have moved off line and literally rolled along the attacker's arm to end up shoulder to shoulder with the attacker and facing in the same direction. Instead of the more "normal" reaction of struggling or fighting at the point of contact, the wrist, I am right beside the attacker and in a better position to understand the direction and power of the attack. I can therefore move more appropriately.

In this aikido example, my getting out of the way of the attack causes the attacker to become off balance and uncentered. It becomes easier to move him in a way that neutralizes the attack.

## GETTING TO THE SOURCE

In creatively resolving those everyday fights at home or in the office, the willingness to understand the other side is essential. Have you ever been in a conflict that only gets worse as you debate the other side? Have you ever been in a conflict—with your parents or children, or a guy in a bar—that ends in frustration for all, as each side digs deeper into its own defensive trench and becomes more rigidly locked into its position? It's not so difficult to comprehend why international skirmishes and violence occur, when we witness full-scale family warfare over putting down the toilet seat.

Emotional issues such as the buildup of nuclear weapons can degenerate into contests in which we spend all our time and mental power defending our position or attacking the other person's. The intellect is burned up in trying to be right. As long as we are involved at the level of the issue, we never understand the other side. Doves and hawks both get to be "right," as one talks of peace and the other talks of strength, but neither is communicating with the other.

Terms such as peace and strength remain ambiguous and undefined. Often we do not attempt to develop and communicate in a common language. Even within our own families, we rarely have the same internal representation of various words. To one person the word *run* means health, jog, fun. To another the word conjures up images of shinsplints, boredom, and agony. Someone else sees elections, politicians, and handshakes—or another stocking ruined!

Let's say Joe, the hawk, and Betty, the dove, are caught up in the nuclear debate. Instead of arguing *ad nauseam* over numbers or types of weapons, Betty realizes she has another choice. She practices the appreciation exercise. She moves off her position to inquire honestly and sincerely about the feelings, interests, and beliefs that led Joe to his pronuclear stand. In the ensuing dialogue, she encourages him to speak of his interests and vision.

"What I'm really interested in is security. I believe that everyone has the right to work toward what they want. I feel deeply about the health and well-being of my children. I envision a world in which my children and my children's children can be secure and safe to grow and to learn and to be happy."

It doesn't take long for Betty to find natural commonality of thought between her and Joe. She also wants a world that's secure and full of opportunity for her children and grandchildren of the future. Joe and Betty begin to understand each other, and to be understood. Moving off of the "right-and-wrong" game, they begin to recognize commonalities and to develop specific solutions to the issues over which they differ. Chapter 9 of this book will cover the topic of cocreation and solution finding.

Roger Fisher and William Ury, in their book *Getting to Yes*, state "It is not enough to know that they see things differently. If you want to influence them, you also need to understand empathetically the power of their point of view and to feel the emotional force with which they believe in it."[27] Being willing to understand is your chance to embrace all aspects of a conflict, not just the positions, but also the feelings, the beliefs, and the interests that both sides have.

Also in *Getting to Yes*, Fisher and Ury tell the story of an interview with President Nasser of Egypt conducted by an American lawyer in 1970. He asked Nasser, "What is it you want Golda Meir to do?"

Nasser replied, "Withdraw from every inch of Arab territory!"

"Without a deal? With nothing from you?" the American asked incredulously.

"Nothing. It's our territory. She should promise to withdraw," Nasser replied.

The American asked, "What would happen to Golda Meir if tomorrow morning she appeared on Israeli radio and television and said, 'On behalf of the people of Israel I hereby promise to withdraw from every inch of territory occupied in '67: the Sinai, Gaza, the West Bank, Jerusalem, the Golan Heights. And I want you to know, I have no commitment of any kind from any Arab whatsoever.' "

Nasser burst out laughing, "Oh, would she have trouble at home!"

Reflecting on this seemingly insignificant dialogue actually increased Nasser's understanding of what an unrealistic option Egypt had been offering Israel. It may have contributed to Nasser's stated willingness later that day to accept a cease-fire in the war of attrition.[28]

If we are willing to move from our initial position—and it only takes one side to do that—we will begin to move the conflict from opposition to understanding.

To illustrate this point to yourself, try this simple exercise. Point your forefingers at each other, then bring them together and start pushing strongly. Almost instantly you are at your limit of pain and tension. Now, maintaining pressure, relax one of them, letting it turn away from you. The other automatically comes alongside the one that relaxed, joining it in pointing out a new direction.

## UNDERSTANDING BEGINS AT HOME

Take any normal conflict that may occur at home, such as Joe Baggodonuts trying to get his young daughter, Bertha, to go to bed on time. Usually this great debate (which we have all experienced as parents and children) becomes a classic case of focusing only on the issue and each person's position on it. Understanding degenerates as the debate progresses.

"Bertha, you need to get to bed."

"Come on, Dad, can't I stay up a little later?"

"No, it's late. Nine o'clock is your bedtime. Now get to bed."

"Why, Dad? You get to stay up late."

"Because I'm grown up. You need rest."

"But I do get rest. I'm not as tired as you, Dad, during the day."

"Bertha, I don't want to argue. Now get to bed."

"Well, I don't think it's fair, Dad. Let me stay up for just a little longer."

"Bertha, I don't want to hear another word out of you. *Now get to bed.*"

Do you recognize this exchange? It can go on for a long time, can't it? Both parties end up frustrated or angry. In such arguments, neither gets off the issue—going to bed. They could spend all day arguing the pros and cons of staying up or going to bed to no avail. So the parent has to use his authority and power to end the argument. (A similar scenario occurs, usually on a subtler level, in the office, with the boss wielding his power over his employees.) But the fight in their minds goes on. Each is fervently debating his side, wanting to be right. It really only takes one person to stop it—he or she just has to give up this type of fight long enough to really understand where that other person is coming from.

Joe might have said, "Bertha, I understand that you do want to stay up later. How much later and why?"

"Well, I want to finish watching this show. It's only a half-hour more. It's really funny."

"I'm just concerned that you get lots of rest. I believe that the healthier you are, the happier you'll be. But I can understand that watching a funny show can make you happy too!" If it feels right, he may even join her in enjoying the show.

"Thanks, Dad. I'll go right to bed after and not dawdle in the bathroom like I usually do."

The conversation can take many different forms. When they communicate with a true willingness to understand, Bertha and Joe will begin to communicate feelings, interests, and beliefs, not just positions on the issue. The more we move away from our position, the closer we will get to what our bigger vision and interests are. This movement enables us to begin to see, hear, and feel similarities between us.

A powerful approach to promoting understanding in a conflict is to focus on asking questions and listening rather than on giving answers or solutions. A sincerely asked question does not leave you as vulnerable to an attack as uninformed position-taking and will increase the rapport simply because you are acknowledging the other person as someone worth listening to.

Asking questions can also help you stay out of possible conflicts. An employee who is burned out and who walks into his boss's office and demands a vacation is likely to get a very different response than an employee who initiates the discussion by asking the boss for his thoughts on the relationship between efficiency and burnout, and for some possible ways of handling it.

## SEEING RED

In 1985, I had the extraordinary opportunity of visiting the Soviet Union with John Denver on a cultural and peace exchange-mission. We Americans have felt so separated from the Soviet people because there has been so little exchange, culturally or economically, between our countries. The only time we see the Soviets is in the newspapers, or in our minds as some dangerous, angry, aggressive villains with fangs, painted red.

My visit to the Soviet Union reminded me of high school or college football days, when I envisioned the other team as a pack of wild monsters with an evil intent to do me harm. When I saw them from a distance on the field, warming up, they looked bigger and stronger and meaner and more evil than I could imagine. When I got up close on the line of scrimmage, when the game actually started and I was dealing with them nose to nose, eye to eye, I saw something different.

I saw there was a boy just like me hidden inside all that protective clothing. He was just a human being, and my potential to be friends with him was as strong as my potential to be friends with any of my own teammates. We had just happened to grow up in a different area and to go to a different school. The only *real* difference was the color of our uniforms.

I had the same feeling in the Soviet Union—in Leningrad, in Moscow, in Talin—sitting, eating, hugging, talking, and sharing life with the Soviets. The bearlike image disappeared as I saw people who were very similar to me. They had two arms and two legs, a brain—they even looked like me. They had children who laughed and cried and played and trusted me. There were grandparents and parents sharing love, hope, and fellowship. They had the same fears as I did and the same basic needs.

As singer-songwriter Jimmy Buffet puts it, "What all people want is to work hard, come home, have a beer, and not get blown up." When I first arrived in the USSR, I felt as if I were in a different neighborhood, around people wearing different-colored jerseys, who played on a different team from me. As we interacted face to face, the differences faded and what stood out were the tears and laughter, fear and love that all humans experience. What stood out was our common humanity.

The simple principle of being willing to understand was working marvelously. As I walked through Leningrad Memorial, an area equivalent to six football fields in size, containing the graves of 600,000 people who died during the siege of Leningrad in World War II, I saw old men and women in civilian clothes, still wearing their medals. I realized that the Soviets were a people who had lost 20 million family members in World War II and who had been involved in one war or another for most of the twentieth century. They had a great desire for peace and a feeling of "Never again" as they prayed for their dead. I saw the Soviets as a strong people with great resolve, very similar, in that regard, to people in the United States. In fact, I got the sense that we were just two brothers with an ongoing sibling rivalry.

I began to consider that in all my years of primary and secondary schooling, there was never a course available to nurture my understanding of the Soviets. I felt hampered by an inability to converse with them in their own language. Remembering that there were more teachers of English in the Soviet Union than there were students of Russian in the United States, I wondered about our country's commitment to understanding these people, and I began to ponder ways to effectively communicate.

Because of the language barrier, it was a challenge for me to articulate my feelings to the Soviets. I found that the smile and the touch and the feeling of being centered and the flow of *ki* said more than language. I also discovered that the Aiki Approach worked very well in communicating powerfully our common dilemma, our actual fear and insecurity. Addressing a group of Soviet educators on the question of U.S.–USSR relations, I asked for a Soviet to assist me in my explanation. I put my fist out to meet his fist. As our fists touched, I started to push. He immediately pushed back. Naturally. He didn't have to think about it. Instead of letting himself be pushed over, he started to push back. This, I explained, was the natural reaction that we all have toward pressure. Humans tend to meet force with force. The harder I pushed, the harder he pushed, without thinking about it. When I asked him whether he felt this had any relevance to American-Soviet relations, he answered, "Yes, most definitely."

I then asked the Soviet to put his face within inches of his fist, and I put my face within inches of my fist and pushed even harder. I said, "Now, how does that feel?" He looked at me and with his Russian accent said, "Not good! *Nyet!*" Everyone laughed. We all knew that this was exactly the absurd position that Americans and Soviets have put themselves in. Pushing harder and harder, and only increasing the fear of hitting one another.

Then, still pushing, I moved my fist down one knuckle so we only had three of the four knuckles touching. Our position was even more precarious. I explained, "Each year we have increased our insecurity. Let's feel this by reducing our connection by one knuckle each time." When we got down to just one knuckle, the chance of slippage was extremely high, and face to face as we were, it was a very insecure feeling. I said, "Now, how does this feel?" His expression said it all: *I don't like this.*

I looked at him and said, "Neither do I. Why are we increasing our insecurity each year with each other?" I then inquired, "What would happen if one of us slipped? Who would be injured?" The answer, of course, was obvious. "Both. It wouldn't matter who created the accident." Very few words needed to be spoken to get the message across. We have created insecurity through a lack of understanding and exchange and through the incessant increase in our military buildup, a real-life nightmare of force against force.

All of us, hawks *and* doves, Republicans and Democrats, communists and capitalists, are interested in security. The common question is, "What is true security?" I next put my fingers in the shape of a gun and placed them at his temple. I asked, "Now how does it feel, if this were a loaded gun?" He again said, "Terrible, not good." I said, "Let me ask you something. Would you like me to be more secure when I'm holding a gun at your temple like this, or less secure?" At that I began to shake, very nervously. It took no time for him to reply, "More secure. Please become most secure." I said, "That is always the question we need to ask ourselves, because in the present world our conflict and our ability to wage war on one another are at such a high technological level that it is as if we each have a gun touching our temples. It's really even worse than that." And I had him put his fingers in the shape of a gun and point it at my temple. The two of us stood there facing each other with our "guns" touching each other's temples. I then turned to the audience and said, "Let's say that this room consists of the world community and that these guns are so destructive that if they go off, everyone in the room also suffers. Which way would you like us to be, more secure or less secure?"

In fact, all national defense decisions should answer the critical question, "Is our policy going to make our neighbors (or 'enemies,' to use the more accepted form) more secure or less secure?" If we are interested in national security, is it in our best interest to have the Soviets feel more secure or less secure? That question needs to be asked constantly if we are to understand and to make appropriate national security decisions.

Whenever I do this fist-and-gun demonstration with citizens of other countries, I realize that the message comes across as powerfully as it does when I do it in a workshop in the United States.

Language is transcended and the communication is clear. The effectiveness of your communication is measured by the response you get. The response I receive is clear and profound—it is a critical time in human history for us to understand one another.

The Aiki principles give us a method for constantly shifting our way of operating, our way of teaching, our way of communicating. Nuclear technology has made war obsolete. Instead of fearing this nuclear technology, we should acknowledge it as one of the best opportunities around to bring the entire world together in cooperation and understanding.

A very relevant analogy to the nuclear arms race is two people sitting in a puddle of gasoline, spending their time, money, and energy making matches. A vivid picture, isn't it? Much of the nuclear debate and the solutions offered today focus on the matches: what to do about the number of matches and the need to reduce or eliminate the matches. The Aiki Approach works on draining the gasoline —reducing the fear and separation that are so prevalent today, and replacing them with acceptance, understanding, and a spirit of cooperation.

When the nuclear power plant at Chernobyl exploded in April 1986, the reaction of people in the United States was not that of enemies but of fellow human beings. Immediate offers of technological aid and medical expertise were made. Dr. Robert Gale of the UCLA Medical Center spent several weeks in the Soviet Union working with Russian medical teams, doing bone marrow transplants for the most critically ill victims of the disaster. The veil of politics was dropped momentarily, and we saw men, women, and children like ourselves in need of our help.

We often think that this is difficult or impossible, or that U.S.–USSR differences are irreconcilable and a long-lasting problem we can do little about. But there have been times in our history when we have totally shifted our perspective and our relationship with another country, primarily through increased understanding. One example is the relationship between the United States and the People's Republic of China.

During the 1950s and 60s, the average American had as great a fear of the "Red Chinese" as we have in the 1980s of the Soviets. At any moment there was the possibility, so we felt, that great numbers of the "Red Mongol hordes" would sweep over our country. But a major shift in attitude occurred sometime during the 1970s. As with all major contextual shifts, we were unaware of it until it was upon us. We suddenly find ourselves in the 1980s with a very warm, congenial attitude toward the Chinese. You ask any cab driver in New York City or Des Moines, Iowa, about the Chinese and they tend to say something like "Oh, those people are magnificent. I just saw those Chinese acrobats on TV the other day. They're fantastic people, the Chinese, those acrobatic, communal living, Ping-Pong playing, gymnastically talented, hard-working Chinese. I love those people. And wasn't it great that the first person to win a gold medal in the 1984 Olympics was Chinese?" And on and on. These are Americans talking about the Red Chinese!

What happened? What created this shift? Certainly you can talk about the Ping-Pong diplomacy of Richard Nixon and his administration in the early seventies. But the overall effect came because we started to open ourselves up to understanding the Chinese through the exchange of people, of business, of culture. We found out that there is much we can do together. For me, one of the great symbols of that shift was an eighteen-hole championship golf course I saw being built in Beijing in the summer of 1985. Can you imagine—golf in the People's Republic?

Yes, we still have weapons pointed at the People's Republic, and they have enough weapons aimed at us to eliminate half of the United States. Yet people don't speak of the need for nuclear reduction talks with the Chinese. Why? The gasoline of tension and fear and insecurity has been drained from Chinese–American relations. We no longer feel or act as if the other were the dreaded bogeyman, waiting to catch us unaware on a dark night.

*With the splitting of the atom, everything has changed save our mode of thinking. Thus we hurl ourselves toward unparalleled catastrophe.*

Albert Einstein

# CONCERT AIKI

In the midseventies, John Denver was planning to embark on a major U.S. tour in which he would perform in a unique setup—in the round. In the middle of packed houses of eighteen thousand or more people, he would be on a small two-foot-high stage, approximately thirty feet in diameter, with people seated around him starting only two or three feet from the stage. As with most famous people, security was a constant concern. John felt that by working together, we could discover a solution that was also in alignment with the Aiki philosophy.

A typical rock concert would never try such an absurd arrangement, given the problems with fans. Given John's popularity, we weren't at all convinced that such an idea was safe. But considering the Aiki philosophy, it was apparent that the quality of John's performance and the quality of his communication on stage should not attract the negative hostile behavior often seen at large concerts. We decided to take a risk to achieve our goal of creating a comfortable "living room" feeling in a very large auditorium: to dispense with traditional concert security measures such as police, uniformed guards, or "bouncers" around the stage. It seems that the greater the security and barriers, the more intense the audience's desire to reach the stage. People love to be challenged.

We felt that by properly preparing the arena personnel and including them in our plans, we could eliminate potential problems before they arose. Consciousness, awareness, and gentleness would be the keys. So with a certain amount of trepidation, I listed all the things that needed to happen. Most important for me was to understand the existing mind-set of most large arena personnel. They often deal with people who are strung out on drugs, drunk, or upset because they don't have the right seat or can't hear the music, or with ardent fans who must get to the stage at all costs. Since the building manager, security people, local police, and ushers control the general house, it was critical they understood they were included as real participants in the show. Two hours before each concert was to begin, we held a meeting with the head of the arena, the head of the ushers, and the head of all the police and security and explained how John performed. We explained the differences between what we were going for and the typical rock concert and asked them for their support and their participation, as if they were actors in the theater. John would take care of the rest. Amazingly enough, instead of strange looks and a "Who are these guys trying to kid?" attitude, they expressed real gratitude at finally being included and appreciated and at someone understanding the difficulties that they had had in previous concerts. Our willingness to understand led naturally to acknowledging their problems and empathizing with them. They responded in kind with interest, supportiveness, and excitement about the concert.

It was amazing to experience eighteen thousand people in a place like Madison Square Garden and be able to hear a pin drop. It was as if everyone was at home, sitting on a living room sofa and listening to a good friend sing and play the guitar.

The few times we tested the system by putting uniformed security at the corners of the stage were the only times we had difficulty. We discovered that just by suggesting we were separate from the audience and did not allow people to approach the stage, we fed their need to do so. Building a "strong defense" just did not work. Inevitably someone would successfully take up the challenge and get on the stage. It was sometimes difficult to get them off. When we had no uniformed security on the floor at all, no sense that we were separate or wanted to be protected from the crowd, the show worked beautifully. We merely had ushers seated in the front row, near the aisles, to help people find their seats and to ask them politely not to walk in front of the stage when John was singing. I would sit in the front row at each concert, just to handle any unforeseen emergencies that might come up, but I acted as if I were a paying customer.

We let go of the urge to just tell the staff what to do. Instead, we took the time to communicate our vision to people, to understand any considerations they might have, and to acknowledge them for the important role they played in manifesting that vision, and they gave us their full support and enthusiasm. Our vision had become theirs.

# Risk Takers

*Before you hit the jackpot, you have to put a coin in the machine.*
Flip Wilson

● Have you ever had difficulty driving or parking a car, or been in a situation in which there were people around who were irritated, waiting for you or yelling at you to do something right? The next time this happens, try yelling at yourself as loud as they would. If you are having trouble parallel parking and there are irritated spectators around, say things such as "What kind of a jerk is parking this car? Where did I learn to park, Sears? What a jerk I am." It's important to say it with sincerity, as if you really are yelling at yourself. It's amazing to watch people stop judging you when they hear you judge yourself.

● Do you ever get irritated with your kids when they get very messy or eat sloppily? Instead of getting upset, try being sloppier than they are. Or if they are eating with their hands, in a restaurant or at home, try putting down your fork and just put your whole face in the plate. Your children might be as disgusted with you as you were with them.

● When you are in an argument with a friend, listen very carefully to what he or she has to say. When there is a pause, ask if you can repeat to him or her exactly what you heard. You will be amazed at how this little exercise will sharpen your listening, be a gift of acknowledgment to the other person, and deepen your ability to understand. Because of your example, your friend may want to do the same when you share your side. You may be surprised at how people interpret what you say.

*It's not enough to study them like beetles under a microscope; you need to know what it feels like to be a beetle.*

Roger Fisher and William Ury
*Getting to Yes*

## THE AIKI APPROACH

### Be Willing to Understand

Understanding

—is the gift that comes from listening;

—is asking questions rather than having the answer;

—allows differences to fade and similarities to come forth;

—naturally acknowledges and appreciates the other person;

—moves us from issue to vision;

—creates movement from stalemate to resolution.

*He not busy being born is busy dying.*
Bob Dylan

# 8. Be Willing to Change

Did you ever think, when you held or looked at a beautiful pearl, that its origin was irritation? An oyster, in response to the irritating presence of sand within its shell, creates a thing of beauty. Not only is the conflict resolved but value is created. When we understand that conflict includes the potential for us to create beautiful pearls and contribute to the world and to ourselves, then we begin to open up our shells, less concerned about letting life in. Embracing conflict can become a joy when we know that irritation and frustration can lead to growth and fascination.

The evolution of every living species has been a lesson in change. Witness the aeronautical design of a hawk, the camouflage magic of the chameleon, the killer instinct of the shark, or the pungent defensive scent of the skunk. All living species must adapt to and evolve with their constantly changing environments to flourish. Change in nature is not a philosophical choice. It is a survival choice. It is a choice for growth and flexibility. Conflict is nature's prime motivator for change.

When we fight with our children about a household chore, or with our fellow worker over which approach to take on a particular project, why is it so hard to change our point of view? Most often it is because we are not nearly as interested in resolving the conflict and possibly creating a new pearl as we are in being right. When we perceive conflict as a threat to our ego, our reaction is to defend or attack. All our energy and mind-power are used in the protection of our ego, not in the growth of our being. Fear of failure reigns supreme.

Great hitters like Pete Rose "fail" over two thirds of the time. If they saw their batting average as failure, their desire to go to the plate the next time would be greatly hindered. Ernest Hemingway rewrote the final chapter of A Farewell to Arms thirty-nine times. Abe Lincoln lost nine out of eleven elections. Robert Fulton's steamship was called "Fulton's Folly." If two-year-olds beat themselves up mentally every time they mispronounced a word, we wouldn't have many speaking humans on the planet today.

To the Pete Roses and Abe Lincolns, there is no such thing as failure, only different outcomes. Being able to take every action as a new experience only expands your knowledge and increases your clarity. You joyously treat conflict as the perfect invitation to grow. You are willing to change.

One spring morning, the philosopher George Santayana was wandering through the lecture hall as he spoke to his spellbound students at Harvard. In the many years he had taught there, he had always paced, using pauses in his movement to punctuate his sentences. At one point he paused for a long time before a window as his eyes came to rest on a yellow hedge of forsythia. At last, he turned to his students who were poised to take down his next words.

"Gentlemen, I very much fear that last sentence will never be completed. You see, I have an appointment with April." He walked out of the room, never lecturing regularly again.[29] George Santayana was not afraid of change.

During a physical confrontation, if a person were coming at you with a circular attack, such as swinging a stick or throwing a hook punch or kick at the side of your head, what would your response be? Over my years in the martial arts, I've discovered that most people put up their arms in a sudden and tense motion to protect themselves, and are so frozen by the swing itself that they rarely move from their position. In effect, they are dealing with the attack right at its most powerful point. There are two places where a hurricane's force will not be felt—one is outside its range of power and the other is inside, at the center. In aikido, both responses are available to you. You can move inside or outside the point of power—in this case, the fist or foot. In addition, the aikidoist moves in the same circular direction as the attack itself, so even if contact is made the impact is minimal. The aikidoist is riding the wave of the attack's energy instead of slamming into it. This requires timing and sensitivity to the direction and intensity of the attacker. The Aiki Approach is akin to dance. It's very difficult to waltz with a break dancer. It's important to be willing to move so that we pick up the tempo of an attack in order to transform it into a dance. The desire to dance with energy creates more awareness and connectedness in every situation.

There is an old adage, "When a pickpocket meets a saint, he sees only his pockets." When we get overly concerned in life with defending ourselves from imagined or real attacks by blocking and striking back, we tend to misperceive loving intentions and react in this same tense, fearful mode. Notice that when a friend goes to put his arm around you, the direction of his movement is very similar to a hook punch. If you are training all your life to fight the world around you, what happens when the hugs come? Do you verbally or emotionally take people's heads off and have to apologize later? As we give up the fighting mind and develop the dancing spirit, our timing and our actions become in tune with each situation.

## CHANGE THAT TUNE

Remember when you were a kid and you wanted to get the teacher's goat? You'd get together with the other kids at recess. "Hey Susie, Joe, Pete, come here. Listen, at 10:18, when the teacher turns her back, I'll give a cue and everyone will drop their books, all together. The sound alone will probably give her a heart attack. At least, she'll get upset and something will happen. It'll be great!" So you'd laugh and get all excited and go back into the classroom.

A schoolteacher who understood the Aiki Approach used it effectively in this situation. At 10:18, she was writing on the blackboard, with her back to everyone. *Bang!* Everyone dropped the books. She turned around, calm and relaxed, walked over to her desk, nonchalantly picked up her book, dropped it with a bang, looked up with a smile, and said, "Sorry I'm late."

She chose "I'm with you guys; I'll dance to this tune," instead of "You win and I'm upset," or "You're after me and I'm angry." There was no one for the students to attack. She moved. She was willing to change, to get off line. That ended the attack, because there was no separation. Her willingness to change joyfully transformed the attack into a dance everyone enjoyed.

---

## THE CHANGE EXERCISE

This simple exercise will illustrate how change—getting off your position—can alter the way you look at a conflict. Have another person stand behind you, put her hands on the back of your shoulders, and start gently but consistently pushing you forward so that you must start walking. As you start walking, have her continue increasing the pressure. After several steps, spin to one side, in the same speed or rhythm as the pusher, rolling along your partner's arm, maintaining contact, so that you end up in back, pushing the person who was just pushing you. The exercise demonstrates clearly that as soon as you are willing to get off line and to change, you find yourself in a powerful position of choice.

---

In the change exercise, your partner may be pushing you in a direction in which you do not want to go. The force of conflict doesn't have to come from another person, however; it can come from yourself. It often results from our attachment to money, power, approval, etc. Have you ever been driven to do something you really didn't care about but did because you thought you had to go along? Have you ever done something because "That's the way it is" and there's nothing you can do about it?

When we think of extraordinary people such as St. Francis of Assisi, we often imagine that their lives were always blessed and that they had none of the debilitating conflicts and attachments that we mortals face. Surely St. Francis was always saintly and pure? Then we discover that Francesco di Pietro Bernardone was one of the more raucous, fun-loving, and partying boys in central Italy. And he certainly had his fair share of conflicts. He had nearly died twice in war, and inherited the burden of carrying on his family's business. Then in 1206, after a day of haggling and bargaining in his role as a successful young merchant, he gave all the money he had made and the clothes off his back to his father. Owning nothing and walking free, the earth became St. Francis' home and all living creations his brothers.

When philosopher-priest Thomas Merton was a young man, he found himself eating scrambled eggs with his friends after another one of his many all-night parties of drinking, smoking, and idle talk. The gnawing desire to do something more to create value from the clutter and debris of his life suddenly broke through. An idea came to him with great clarity, and he stated, amidst the eggs, coffee, and smoke, "You know, I think I ought to enter a monastery and become a priest."[30] Many of us have made similar statements under the influence of guilt or spirit. The incredible thing is that Thomas Merton put out his cigarette and did it.

Change does not take time, it takes commitment.

## THE DYNAMICS OF CHANGE

In the diagram on page 158, box #1, labeled "Mind-stuff," represents mind-sets—all your beliefs, knowledge, information. It is the storage bank of your being, where you have filed away in consciousness or unconsciousness your thoughts and your images of the past. From this often-cluttered array, you formulate, either consciously or unconsciously, a personal vision or image of who you are, what you are, and where you are going (box #2).

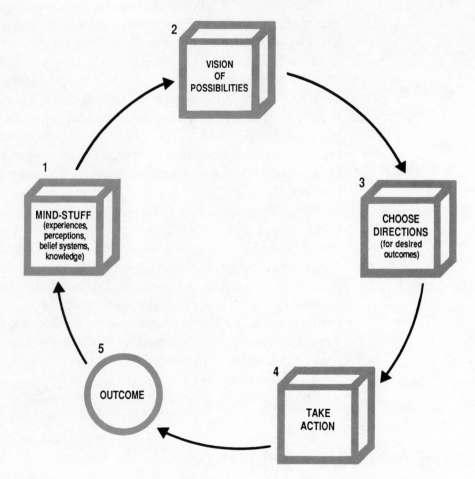

## THE DYNAMICS OF CHANGE

Even the most impoverished wino has a personal vision, whether he is conscious of it or not, that directs his choices and his actions (boxes #3 and 4). The wino's personal vision may be "I am worthless, weak, and addicted." This image permeates his very being and produces the directions he will take in life, and their outcomes (box

#5). If you think you have a bad voice, the least of your priorities in any given day is to stand up in front of a crowd at a local shopping mall and break into song, or to apply for a job as lead singer in a local music group.

So your choice of directions emerges from your personal vision. And from those directions, or for those desired outcomes, you take action. You do *something*, whether it's seeking a fifth of whiskey, painting a picture, starting a business, or working to end world hunger. The action that you undertake produces an actual outcome. It is right here, at the actual outcome, that conflicts usually emerge. Conflicts are often the perception of a difference between the actual outcome and the chosen direction, or between the actual outcome and the overall vision. When the actual outcome does not meet our expectations, we are left with an interesting choice. Responding positively leads to expansion and growth; reacting negatively, to contraction and depression. Although both will result in change, your willingness to change will inevitably affect the result and the quality of your life.

When Glen Cunningham was seven years old, his legs were severely burned in a tragic fire. Medical experts said he would never walk again. His doctor recommended that Glen's legs be amputated if he survived the initial shock. For the next six weeks, it was not a question of walking, it was a question of just surviving. When Glen was finally able to sit up in bed, the condition of his legs was a shock to him. His left foot was missing most of the toes, as well as the ball of the foot. The right leg was bent and shorter than the left. And the pain would not go away. Clearly, this predicament was not Glen's original choice of direction. Glen made a decision. He would use this as an opportunity to commit to positive change. He would not give up. Three years later, he gave up his crutches. He found that by "sort of running or hippety-hopping along," he could forget about the pain. He never stopped running. In 1938 he stunned the sports world with a world-record mile-time of 4 minutes, 4.4 seconds. And to Roger Bannister and all the others who have broken the four-minute mile, Glen Cunningham has been a legend and an inspiration. And he is even more than that to the many thousands of troubled youngsters who since the 1940s have had the opportunity for change, in working with Glen and his wife on their ranch in Kansas.[31]

## THE DEPRESSION SPIRAL

When our outcomes do not meet with our expectations, and we feel we have failed and are not worthy, we move into a contracting spiral. It is based on our need to prove that we are not bad and not a failure. The survival of our ego is at stake. Our vision begins to be stated in things we don't want—"I don't want to fail," "I don't want to be unhealthy," or "I don't want to be poor." Our motivation is based on fearfully moving away from those things we don't want rather than moving toward those things we do want. If a baseball player strikes out, and associates this with not being a worthy person, often his immediate reaction is to blame something or someone (the light, the umpire, himself). Our personal vision and ego is perceived to be threatened. Our new desired outcome is to defend ourselves, our ego, or to attack whatever it is that we perceive as causing our failure. This produces jealousy, blame, self-justification, anger, fear, or the need to run away, which in turn escalates the original conflict. This causes us to go into an ever-tightening spiral of ego survival, depression, and contraction—until we recognize the folly of entering into this black hole of separateness. This spiral has been felt not just by the down-and-out street folks, but by those at the pinnacle of success, as is evident in the tragic deaths of such people as Marilyn Monroe, John Belushi, and Janis Joplin. The trappings of success show externally, but internally the downward spiral is being tightly wound.

*The only person who likes change is a wet baby.*
Roy Z-M Blitzer

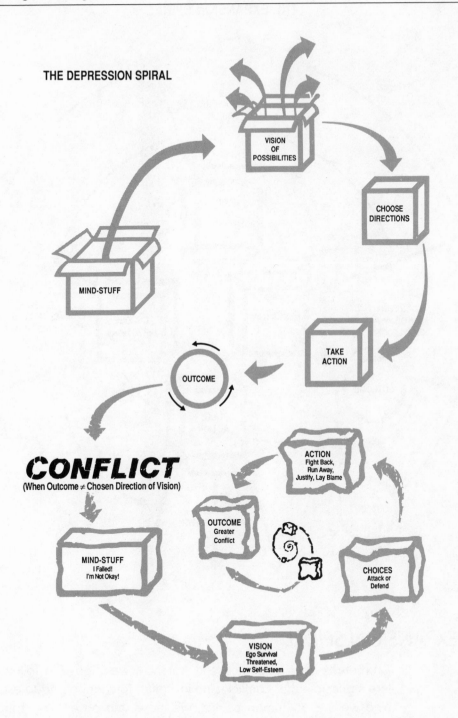

**THE DEPRESSION SPIRAL**

VISION
OF
POSSIBILITIES

CHOOSE
DIRECTIONS

MIND-STUFF

TAKE
ACTION

OUTCOME

**CONFLICT**
(When Outcome ≠ Chosen Direction of Vision)

ACTION
Fight Back,
Run Away,
Justify, Lay Blame

OUTCOME
Greater
Conflict

MIND-STUFF
I Failed!
I'm Not Okay!

CHOICES
Attack or
Defend

VISION
Ego Survival
Threatened,
Low Self-Esteem

# THE EXPANSION SPIRAL

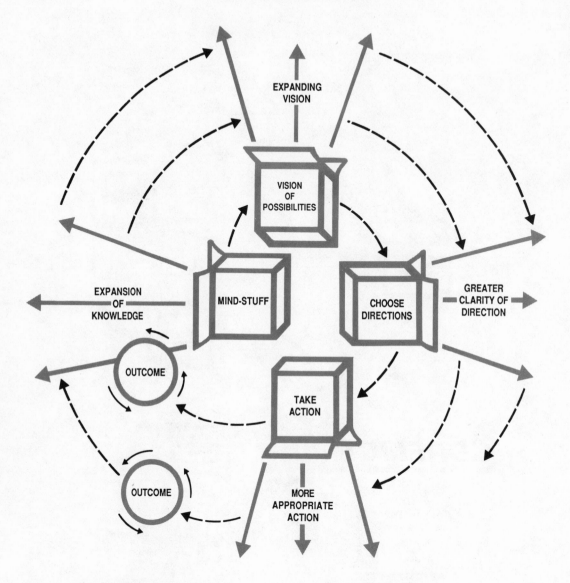

*Diagram labels:*
- EXPANDING VISION
- VISION OF POSSIBILITIES
- MIND-STUFF
- CHOOSE DIRECTIONS
- GREATER CLARITY OF DIRECTION
- EXPANSION OF KNOWLEDGE
- OUTCOME
- TAKE ACTION
- OUTCOME
- MORE APPROPRIATE ACTION

## *THE EXPANSION SPIRAL*

There is another choice, fortunately. If we choose to follow nature's principle that conflict is an invitation to change and to expand who we are as human beings, we move into an exciting spiral of growth and creativity. Since all action leads to experience, and experience is the foundation for learning, we begin to recognize that all outcomes, whether they do or do not meet our expectations, expand our ability to know. We begin to recognize that the more we know, the more potential we have for a greater and clearer vision. We can then formulate clearer and more specific choices about our directions. As a result, we will take more appropriate and focused action to produce those outcomes we desire.

Let's look at the example of a baseball player who has a personal vision that says "I can hit." His choice of direction will obviously be to get a base hit. His action is to pick up the bat, go to the plate, and swing the bat at the ball. Let's say his actual outcome is to strike out. Obviously there is a conflict. His desired outcome, to get a hit, did not happen. Instead of saying, "I failed and failure is bad," he recognizes that his actual experience or outcome produced more knowledge. He now knows better what a curve ball looks like, as well as the fast ball he expected. His knowledge has expanded, and therefore his vision "I can hit," which is based on his belief "I can hit what I can see" or "I can hit what I can know," has now expanded. His desired outcome, to get a hit, becomes even greater, his action even more enthusiastic and directed. If he strikes out on a slider the next time, his knowledge increases again, as do his vision of possibilities and his new desire and skill. Regardless of the outcome, he knows he is making progress toward greater understanding and therefore getting closer to achieving his goals.

In 1986, Mel Fisher discovered the Spanish galleon *Atocha* on the ocean floor forty-five miles off the coast of Florida. The *Atocha* contained over $400 million in gold and silver. This ended a seventeen-year search that had left him bankrupt and embroiled in lawsuits, and his son and daughter-in-law dead in shipwrecks.

Every morning of those seventeen years, Mel Fisher bounded out of bed and shouted, "Today's the Day!" It gave him energy, powerfully reminded him of his vision, and inspired his crew toward their dream. Each new day he was choosing the expansion spiral.

We have a choice when we are not getting what we want in life —the expansion spiral of learning and growth, or the depression spiral of escalating conflict. The expansion spiral is ours if we are willing to change, and have the behavioral flexibility to continue learning and trying new things, to do whatever it takes. We are able to shift frustration into fascination, and alarm or concern into awareness and knowledge. To succeed in our vision, we must take action. Since taking action leads to the possibility of failure, it is easy to see why so many of us do not manifest our vision. We choose to contract or depress, and become afraid to take action since it might potentially show us up as failures. When we are willing to change, the concept of failure fades. We begin to understand that all action produces greater learning and experience. We are able to continually proceed, to let go of fear and hold fast to our vision.

The choice we make between the depression spiral and the expansion spiral is often predicated on whether or not our motivation to change is based on moving toward something we love or away from something we fear. The Australians had never won the world's most prestigious sailing event, the America's Cup. Australian captain John Bertrand was more than willing to change all of that. His motivation was toward something he loved dearly, sailing to victory with a team totally committed to excellence and to each other. Instead of focusing on the years of past losing, he gave his crew a simple vision. "We are going to sail this boat as boats will be sailed in the year 2000, as no crew has ever sailed a boat before." Knowing that teamwork required a willingness to get off of your own position for the sake of a bigger vision, he had his team commit themselves to living together for two years and to having a visualization session each day, of winning the Cup together. They would see, hear, taste, and feel every aspect of the race. Two years of this made the vision a reality—they won the 1983 America's Cup.[32] In 1987, the American team, under the direction of Dennis Conner, had a similar vision and victory.

What drives you, fear or love? Have you ever asked yourself, as you clench your teeth and climb relentlessly uphill in life, whether your motivation comes from the great love you have for doing what you do, or whether it comes from the fear of losing someone's approval, like that of your parents, friends, or even God?

In the early 1980s, Nancy Hogshead was burned out from swimming. In 1977, at the tender age of fourteen, she was ranked number one in the world in the butterfly and held two American records. She had put herself under tremendous pressure to win all the time. In the late 1970s she began to be aware that she had not been listening to her body or her feelings. She had been having frequent injuries and sickness, but her desire to please others had allowed her to push on. By 1981 she recognized that she was not consciously choosing any of this, the pain or the fame. She took a very courageous step (especially since it looked like a show of weakness) and dropped out of competition completely for over a year and a half.

"During that period of time, I became a couch potato. I never once got into a pool. I needed to discover who I was and what I really wanted."

Only eighteen months before the 1984 Olympics, Nancy decided that swimming was a special gift that she had and that she could choose to do it for the joy and fun of it. From then on she would take responsibility and would define success internally rather than through someone else's eyes.

"For the first time, swimming became fun. I was not doing it out of fear of losing someone's approval, but instead, out of the love for the special gift that God had given me and for the purpose of becoming all that I could be," Nancy explained to me.

In the 1984 Olympics, she included in her fun three gold medals. By choosing to move "beyond the gold," toward love for what she was doing, the gold came to her in triplicate.

*My goal in life is to unite my avocation with my vocation*
    *As my two eyes make one in sight.*
*For only where love and need are one*
    *And work is play for mortal stakes*
*Is the deed ever really done*
    *For heaven's and for future's sake.*

                                        Robert Frost

## TAKING THE HIGHER GROUND: MOVING FROM A POINT OF VIEW TO A VIEWING POINT

When I'm hiking in the mountains, I often find myself on densely wooded trails, not quite sure where I am or where I am going. It expands my perception and perspective dramatically to climb a tree or a ridge to take a look not only at my point on the path, but also at my point's relation to other places along the path. In a conflict, being willing to change allows you to move from a point of view to a viewing point—a higher, more expansive place, from which you can see both sides.

A point of view often is something we need to defend. A viewing point is a place of increased perspective and greater possibilities. Rising up to a viewing point takes only one person. It doesn't require movement on the other person's part. Rising up to a viewing point does not mean totally forsaking your point of view. It puts your point of view in perspective, in relation to the whole.

When H. G. Wells wrote *The War of the Worlds,* he established a point of view for millions that alien beings are killers and a threat to humanity. More than fifty years later, Steven Spielberg gave us another perspective by creating the lovable E.T. and by showing the possibility of friendly, benevolent aliens. Given this new viewing point, suddenly children throughout the world are hoping for an invasion of aliens and even adults are scanning the heavens with a new perspective.

Establishing a viewing point provides us with more objective criteria through which we can move off of stalemates and resolve conflicts. During the International Law of the Sea Conference, India, representing the Third World bloc, proposed that a $60 million initial fee be charged to companies desiring to do deep-seabed mining. The United States proposed that there be no initial fee. Both countries refused to budge. Their individual points of view rose to a new viewing point when it was discovered that the Massachusetts Institute of Technology had created a model for the economics of deep-seabed mining. This model was gradually accepted by both parties as objective and provided a way of evaluating each of their proposals. India was able to realize that its proposal made it prohibitive for any company to mine, and the United States, whose previous proposal was based only on information from mining companies, saw the importance of some initial fee. As a result of this viewing point, both countries moved off of their positions and a settlement was reached.[33]

As parents, our willingness to move from our position or attitude can be very nurturing and empowering for a child. There are so many safety issues where a child does not have the ability to make decisions on his own. But there are many nonthreatening situations where we can lighten up and be willing to change, abandon control positions, and allow the child to choose and become empowered. Any two-year-old provides us with an excellent opportunity to do this. There she is, as willful as you can imagine, but certainly not bad or evil. She is exploring her need for choice and power and control. But she's just learning. She's not as good or as subtle as we are yet. That's why she tends to be more obnoxious. As we get caught up in keeping her from those things we should keep her from—running out in the street or going near deep water or grabbing that Doberman by the tail—sometimes we let the responsible parent within us get carried away. We find ourselves reacting in the same overprotective way to almost everything she does. As we expand our perspective and move to a higher viewing point, we begin to see her as a magical child intent on controlling her movement and making conscious choices. We're willing to be more flexible and supportive of this important learning time. Maybe we'll even find it's OK if she wants to wear her dress backwards or the pink sock with the red one.

Change is often risky. In order to risk, it is important to take ourselves more lightly. We do that naturally in play. When we're playing a game like Monopoly, we can be the shoe or the thimble or the wheelbarrow. We will risk being different and doing different things. We can go for Boardwalk one minute and buy Mediterranean Avenue the next. We're willing to play, to risk trying new things. Change takes on a joyful quality. With this attitude we can take our lives seriously and responsibly, but ourselves more lightly.

Remember when your child was a one-year-old tossing Gerber's peaches on the floor? And just as you went to clean up the mess, you got hit on the head by a falling spoon? And then within seconds, there went the whole plate? There are two distinct ways to perceive the one-year-old's action: as some obnoxious attempt to exasperate the parent, or as an interesting game of watching gravity and Daddy work together, all under the infant's direction. What a great way for that child to acquire personal power and to influence his environment. Your opportunity is to choose a perspective that works, to enjoy, be playful. There is nothing like levity to improve one's perspective.

Be willing to change. If we're not willing to change, we find ourselves getting stuck in patterned reactions that we use over and over, even though the situation may have changed drastically. If a parent's response to a young child spilling his milk is the same as his response to the child striking matches, the child has trouble making distinctions about the true importance of each situation, even though it is obvious to the parent. It is not effective management of our employees if we use the same inflection, volume of voice, and tone of importance for the person who is two minutes late as for the person who consistently comes to work hours late and drunk. Instead of reacting with equal gravity to all situations, our willingness to change will enable us to vary our response. Our communication becomes clearer. Being more flexible allows us to cooperate with those around us and to cocreate solutions that are acceptable to both parties.

## METHODS AND CHANGE

Years ago I had the great fortune to meet an old man who was very wise. He taught me in a way that has proven valuable throughout my life. I was discussing with him a philosophy I was then pursuing that I found very provocative and transforming.

He looked at me with his old, furrowed face, his eyes twinkling beneath bushy eyebrows, and said, "Yes, methods can be useful."

He often had this habit of irritating me by stating the obvious, which inevitably caused me to reply, "So? I know that. Big deal. That's why I'm studying."

Then he looked at me deliberately and said, "Methods are, by definition, traps."

As usual, I had the feeling that I had bitten the lure and there he was, reeling me in. He had all of my interest and attention. "Oh, I know what you mean," I said. "Methods are useful, but you have to be careful. As you use them, you don't want to be trapped by them."

He looked at me with the fatherly look he sometimes gave me and shook his head. "No, that's not what I meant. What I meant was, in order for a method to be truly useful, you must get trapped by it."

Once more, he had me, spinning my head like a top and generally befuddling my mind. Soothing my bewilderment, he put his hand softly on my shoulder and said, "So, my blessing to you is that when you are exploring a method, you do so fully—go for it 100 percent, get trapped by it. But when that method begins to self-destruct, let it go. Don't try to defend it or be evangelical about it, because as those walls around you called your method begin to crumble, your tendency will be to try to hold up the walls to make the method work like you thought it would work. But behind those walls are even more magic and power and"—he paused—"another trap."

"So go for the new method. Enjoy. When those walls around the new method, around the 'new you,' begin to fall and crumble, don't try to hold them up. Let them go, because behind those crumbling walls are true miracles and power and—another trap."

"So go for it 100 percent. And when those walls of the new 'new you' begin to crumble, don't try to hold them up. Let them go because behind them, there are even more magic and power and—another trap. So go for it. . . ."

And on he went, six times, until I was lulled into a deep trance—and trapped.

*All 'graduations' in human development mean the abandonment of a familiar position . . . all growth . . . must come to terms with this fact.*
Erik H. Erikson

## Risk Takers

• Are you uncomfortable around people with physical handicaps? Mental handicaps? How about people of certain races or religions? Old people? Young children? Street people? Examine those situations where you find yourself uncomfortable. Then go out and spend the day being of service to those people. Try to see the world through their eyes.

• When you find yourself in the middle of a heated argument, capitulate, saying something like, "Yes, you're absolutely right. I have no more argument." Look for signs of diminishing anger and openings for building greater rapport.

• If you feel that you are doing the same things over and over again, take a day or an afternoon and change your style of clothing. Go to a new town or a new location where no one knows you. Be that "new you" totally. Return to another age, like fourteen, and go roller skating, have milk shakes. Change things around to break up a defined pattern of activity. Change your eating habits. Change your sleeping habits for a few days. Work all night and sleep during the day. Get up in the middle of the night, work for a couple of hours, and then go back to sleep. Sleep is a good pattern to break because we often have too-sharply-defined boundaries between waking, sleeping, and dreaming. As you change your sleeping habits radically, you'll start to experience great value in having your sense of reality broken down somewhat. Knowing that you can change your perception of reality by choice expands your vision of possibilities and therefore your ability to be flexible.

• Discreetly and subtly match or mirror the movements, body posturing, breathing, tempo, and tonality of someone with whom you are relating. Notice any increase of rapport during this process.

• Pretend that there are no secrets and that everyone knows everything there is to know about you. How much more relaxed and free do you become?

*An idea that isn't risky is hardly worth calling an idea.*
                                                    Oscar Wilde

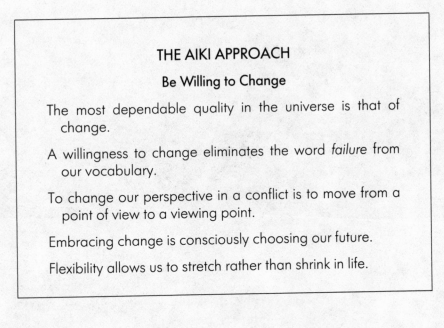

**THE AIKI APPROACH**

**Be Willing to Change**

The most dependable quality in the universe is that of change.

A willingness to change eliminates the word *failure* from our vocabulary.

To change our perspective in a conflict is to move from a point of view to a viewing point.

Embracing change is consciously choosing our future.

Flexibility allows us to stretch rather than shrink in life.

# 9. Choose to Cocreate

*What a strange machine man is! You fill him with bread, wine, fish and radishes, and out of him come sighs, laughter and dreams.*

Nikos Kazantzakis
*Zorba the Greek*

There is an old rabbinic tale which goes:

*And the Lord said to the Rabbi, "Come, I will show you Hell."*

*They entered a room where a group of people sat around a huge pot of stew. Everyone was famished and desperate. Each held a spoon that reached the pot but had a handle so long that it could not be used to reach their mouths. The suffering was terrible.*

*"Come, now I will show you Heaven," the Lord said after a while.*

*They entered another room, identical to the first—the pot of stew, the group of people, the same long spoons. But, there, everyone was happy and nourished.*

*"I don't understand," said the Rabbi. "Why are they happy here when they were miserable in the other room, and everything was the same?"*

*The Lord smiled. "Ah, but don't you see?" he asked. "Here they have learned to feed each other."*[34]

Cocreation is a natural result of accepting our connectedness to the world around us and recognizing its indisputable interdependence. Cocreation is being open to synergistically creating systems that serve the universe of which you are an integral part and that support your overall vision and deep sense of purpose in life.

Choosing cocreation is an obvious step to take in resolving conflict. We all recognize the value of cooperation. So why do we often forget it when conflicts arise in our life? There is one simple reason. It takes time, energy, and work to cocreate when there are major differences in a relationship. It's easier to avoid a problem, or "go along" with the opposing viewpoint (secretly resentful, of course), or simply fight it out. Cocreation takes listening and understanding and a commitment to discovering a solution together. It means not having it be just your way, but rolling up your sleeves to create new possibilities.

Somewhere there is an inventor in his workshop who is brilliant and has an invention he considers excellent. He wants to have it acknowledged and marketed throughout the world. He thinks he needs to do it all. He may have very poor business ability, but because the invention is his, he decides he must market it, he must advertise it, he must do the financial planning and work. His invention takes on such importance that his life becomes a secret mission and he is constantly wary of everyone, thinking them potential enemies out to usurp his plans and ideas. As a result, he will be lucky if he gets his product off his workshop shelf.

The same inability to understand the power of cocreation can hamper a marketing person who, instead of trusting his technicians and giving them the freedom to explore and to develop, always needs to have them under his control to produce the product he wants.

When the inventor sees that someone with financial ability is actually his financial arm, and someone else with advertising ability is his advertising or promotion arm, then he is extending himself beyond his own talents and becoming far richer in ability. When he perceives his support people as an extension of himself, all information gets shared.

With trust, mutual support, and the desire to work with one another, the results people can achieve defy imagination. John F. Kennedy challenged the United States in the early 1960s to put a man on the moon within that decade, and people began working together to produce that common goal. Scientists who considered it impossible enrolled in the effort. They followed the Aiki principle of "embracing tiger," which means to unconditionally and joyfully accept conflict as an opportunity to do the extraordinary. Their entire context shifted from "It can't be done and I don't want to be involved" to "In order for this to be done, these are the problems that need to be solved." People working on the moon project were able to accept differences and use them to their advantage to synergistically produce solutions. Instead of seeing opposition to an idea as a deterrent, the moon project workers were able to consider other workers in opposition as actually being on the same team. As team members, they were there to make sure that the best possible solutions were worked out and that all considerations were handled. The critics became part of the solution rather than part of the problem. Many critics evolved into monitors of quality control.

Scientists, politicians, and the general public embraced a possibility, and their commitment transformed their doubts, their fears and their limitations. Hundreds of thousands of precise processes came together to accomplish a feat that a few years earlier only a handful of bizarre-minded people had considered possible. In 1969, man walked on the moon.

When we perceive differences in personality and abilities as gifts and as pieces of a magnificent puzzle, we put them together to form a masterpiece of power and creation truly larger than anyone's single vision.

When there is a real commitment to a vision that is clearly and positively stated in measurable outcomes, support and ideas arise from everywhere. Cocreation occurs quite naturally.

## Commitment

Until one is committed
there is hesitancy, the chance to draw back,
always ineffectiveness.

Concerning all acts of initiative (and creation)
there is one elementary truth,
the ignorance of which kills countless ideas
and splendid plans:
that the moment one definitely commits oneself,
then Providence moves too.
All sorts of things occur to help one
that would otherwise never have occurred.

A whole stream of events issues from the decision,
raising in one's favor all manner
of unforeseen incidents and meetings
and material assistance,
which no man could have dreamt
would have come his way.

I have learned a deep respect for one of Goethe's couplets:
  'Whatever you can do, or dream you can . . . begin it.
  Boldness has genius, power and magic in it.'

W. N. Murray
*The Scottish Himalayan Expedition—1951*

# A TEST OF STRENGTH

I use a simple demonstration in lectures and workshops to show graphically the power of cocreation. I first let the group know that we are going to do an exercise based on strength and power. I select two volunteers of comparable size and strength for a "strength test" to be done in plain view of everyone. I ask each volunteer to think of five goals or material possessions they would like to have but not to express them out loud.

The rules of the match are as follows:

The time limit of the match is thirty seconds. Each time one person brings his opponent's arm to the table, he will achieve one of his goals. Immediately, the contestants are to bring their arms back to the starting position and the match will commence again. I restate the purpose clearly—this is a winning-through-strength game.

Inevitably, both persons immediately view it as the usual arm wrestling contest. Even after an intensive workshop on true power being based on *ki* and centering, I find both participants reverting to old patterns. They strain and struggle to defeat each other, thinking this is the only way to win and thus achieve their goals. In the thirty seconds, there are usually one or two wins, at most. Often there are none, just a great deal of strain and struggle. After the match, I ask the contestants whether they felt they won or lost and what thoughts they had about the game. Inevitably, they felt they needed to try harder or that they needed a different or better technique.

I then ask them to recall the Aiki principles we have been working on and whether there could be a more powerful way to play the game, to achieve all of their goals. Light bulbs seem to go on everywhere as they recognize the simple solution to achieving their goals. I give them another opportunity, and instead of using the adversarial "you or me" approach, they work together as a team.

Within a few seconds, without struggle, they work together, going back and forth—first one partner's arm down, then the other's—ten times. Whether they are schoolchildren or successful business people, the revelation is the same.

The participants seem to feel a little foolish when they realize how easy it was for them to jump right back into a win/lose approach, in which neither achieved their goals. They become acutely conscious of the awareness necessary to break deeply rooted patterns.

It is valuable to note the distinction between cocreation and compromise. Roger Fisher tells a story that illustrates this difference. There are two people who each want a single orange. They fervently debate who is entitled to the orange. Being fair-minded people, they finally divide the orange in half. The first person, sort of happy that he has half an orange, goes to his house, peels the orange, throws away the peel, and eats the fruit. The second person, sort of happy that he has half an orange, goes to his house, peels the orange, throws away the fruit, and uses the peel to bake a cake.[35]

Compromise. Often in life we are so intent on doing the "fair" thing that we never look at what we are really going for. We never see the possibility that there is enough for each to have everything he or she needs—the possibility that we can do more with less.

Choosing to cocreate has been a major factor in almost all important success stories: in the great sports teams of history, such as the vintage teams of the New York Yankees, Green Bay Packers, and Boston Celtics; in consistently successful companies such as IBM and 3M, and in notable entrepreneurial upstarts such as Apple Computer; in world achievements such as the eradication of smallpox. We do it best when we do it together.

When Ruth Eisenberg met Margaret Patrick, she was feeling very sorry for herself. Ruth had recently suffered a stroke, and while that was bad enough, the worst part was that she could no longer play the piano. Her right hand was still good, but her left was totally useless.

Margaret had been a piano teacher and church organist for fifty years, when a stroke paralyzed her right side. Afterward, she could play the piano with only her left hand. She too lost the central activity in her life until, a little over a year later, she was introduced to Ruth.

"It was a miracle that brought us together," she said. Both had been undergoing therapy at the same senior center for over a month, but didn't meet until Millie McHugh, their program director, saw their potential and introduced them. Ruth, stout, garrulous, and white-haired, was playing the piano with her good hand when Millie walked up with Margaret, a slender, reserved black woman. Margaret and Ruth immediately began talking; after a few minutes, they sat down and, together, played Chopin's Minute Waltz, Ruth on the treble and Margaret on the bass. Soon they were playing together regularly and a strong friendship blossomed around their common love of music. Outwardly so different, they discovered an inner harmony that perfectly complemented their musical partnership.

Within a few months they took their talents "on the road" to other senior centers and hospitals in the New York area and were quickly dubbed "Ebony and Ivory" after the Paul McCartney/Stevie Wonder hit song. And, as in the song, they are "playing together in perfect harmony."[36]

*My name used to be Me. But now it's You.*
**Theophane the Monk**

# WINNING THE AIKI WAY

Winning. It sounds good, doesn't it? It certainly is a powerful word. People are either scared of it, driven by it, or deeply concerned about what it is doing to all of us. If we were to be perfectly honest with ourselves, most of us would admit that when we pick up that tennis racket or golf club or softball we have a strong intent to win, to score the most points, to beat the other guy. Notice the apprehension and stress you feel prior to playing the "big" game. The best way to discover how much this means to you is to notice your reaction and feelings when you lose the match, strike out, or miss that crucial putt. Lose, losing, lost. It even sounds bad.

How about using a little Aiki? First, let's risk looking at what is going on right now. Merely by growing up in today's world, we have undergone a psychophysiological patterning that says winning is good and losing is bad. Often the benefits of playing and competing are negated by the stress we create by beating ourselves up mentally or emotionally at each loss. Think about the anxiety that occurs even before the game because of our deep-rooted fear of losing, and the feeling we have when our success and well-being are dependent upon someone else losing. And worse yet, think of the fun we miss when our anxieties cause us to quit in midstream or deter us from even playing the game in the first place!

As we choose to cocreate, we are able to make more subtle distinctions about our reactions to winning and losing. We begin to notice the stress that we create within ourselves when we think "Winning is everything," or the more anxious version, "I don't want to (or can't afford to) lose." Often we try to fight back the stress directly with thoughts such as "Who cares about winning?" or "I'm playing just to have fun, not to win," or "I don't care if I lose." Since deep inside we often don't believe these statements, we escalate the internal conflict we wanted so much to alleviate.

Rather than trying to beat down persistent thoughts like "Winning is the only thing" with contradictory thoughts, let's play Aiki further. Instead of fighting our tendency to win, let's accept it. If our definition of winning is the traditional one of beating the other person, our chances of winning are reduced if we play someone more skilled than we are. Always winning when it's a point-getting game becomes increasingly difficult as we play more accomplished opponents. As Tim Gallwey,[37] author and lecturer, jokingly tells his workshop participants, "If you really want to win the tennis match all the time, always play someone much worse than you are." But alas, all the enjoyment soon goes out of the sport. Is there really a way to always win and yet keep life enjoyable and challenging?

Certainly. Just re-create what we mean by winning. Expand the possibilities. Instead of fighting this idea of winning, blend with it and see its value.

Look at the gut-level payoffs to winning. It creates a good feeling inside. It's fun and highly energizing. So if it's all that great, why fight it? The more harmonizing approach would be "How do we get more of it?" or "How do we cocreate with the other side so that we both win?" One way is to simply expand our definition of the word "win." Scoring the most points is only one way of winning and creating those good feelings. Those "winning feelings" come about just as often through learning a great deal, developing stronger skills, and laughing a lot. Who do you think grows stronger when there is a tennis match between a more experienced player and a less experienced one? Certainly the less experienced player doesn't win matches as consistently, but who is winning the "strength-progress" game? Or the learning game?

We have the choice to expand our definition of winning to such an extent that the inhibiting action from fear of failure literally disappears. Thomas Edison "failed" over 10,000 times before producing a working light bulb. When asked how he could persist after 9,999 failures, he replied simply, "I did not fail 9,999 times. I succeeded 9,999 times in learning how *not* to make a light bulb."

When tests at the 3M company of a new bonding compound "failed" miserably, management didn't have the normal knee-jerk reaction of tossing it in the trash can. They asked what could be learned from the "failure" and if there were any applications for which the compound could be useful. Secretaries noticed that its "weakness" was actually its strength. It was perfect for attaching temporary notes to objects and leaving those objects unmarred when the notes were removed. Eureka! A multimillion-dollar product, Post-it note pads, was created.

As you expand winning to include all possibilities, you will discover that if you are not winning one game, you are naturally winning another. Every possible outcome in life can provide you with a precious "win." You begin to see that the only things you actually lose are your limited and restrictive belief systems.

As you proceed along this winning path, the person across the net (or across the hall) takes on a different role. He becomes a partner rather than an opponent. When winning does not mean that someone else has to lose, your approach to life becomes a cocreative process. Life becomes "you *and* me" rather than "you *or* me."

Over two hundred studies in recent years have shown conclusively that the long-held belief that competition is the fastest and best way to improve performance or gain excellence is at best inaccurate and at worst false.[38] These studies fly directly in the face of our present attitudes. Success and doing well are synonymous with victory, and for me to be victorious, you must lose. These are the accepted passwords for making it in today's world.

The question that needs to be asked is, "Do we really perform better and feel better when we are trying to beat someone else than when we are cooperating with them or than when we are working alone?" Psychologist Robert Helmreich of the University of Texas has conducted extensive studies since the late 1970s on seven different groups, including scientists, college undergraduates, elementary school students, airline pilots, and business people. In each of these widely different groups, competitiveness was associated with poorer performance. Helmreich found the study on business people particularly interesting because of the common assumption that competition is good for business. It was discovered that when we put all that much attention or energy into beating someone else, we do not focus as well on the job at hand. Performance and quality often go downhill. In another eye-opening study of business people by Helmreich, salary was used as the measure of achievement. There was an inverse relationship between competitiveness and achievement—i.e., between competitive tendencies and salary level.

It is also interesting to note that the case against emphasizing competition in education has been strengthened considerably. A large body of research by David and Roger Johnson, professors of education at the University of Minnesota, showed conclusively in nearly two hundred studies over a ten-year period that cooperation promoted higher achievement in *all* subject areas and *all* age groups than competition or independent work. Those old familiar classroom shouts of "Do your own work!" or "No helping!" that sent shivers down our spines may be dinosaurs looking for permission to die. Children simply do not learn better when placed in a competitive system.

The two dominant models of our present educational system have been competition and individualized learning. Even though cooperation has proven to be by far the better system, it may take some very creative educators to initiate it into the system. It is such an alien concept within most schools that a typical observer noticing such behavior might wonder why "it's OK for all those kids to cheat." New cooperative models are proving very successful. One is based on the "jigsaw" method, in which each person is given a piece of information and must cooperate with the entire group to come up with a complete report. Another less structured model is to have a group come up with as many alternatives as possible, such as how many things they can find that affect the burning time of a candle.

And does cooperation help the less able children at the expense of the more gifted ones? Studies have shown that when groups of students of varied abilities come together to help one another, with the goal being that everyone in the group must know how to solve the problem, both gifted and less able students prosper. The old cliché that the teacher learns as much as the student proves itself out. And maybe even more important, study results show that students have more fun in the cooperative mode. In fact, the Johnsons cite seven studies since 1984 that indicate people often say they enjoy competition but then change their minds when they experience what it is like to work and play in a setting that does not require winners and losers.

If the power of cooperation takes its appropriate place as the new paradigm in business and education, this world will change dramatically. Instead of hoping to see each other fail, we will be pulling for each other to succeed. "We need all of us" will become a rallying cry for creating a powerful, healthy, and peaceful world.

*In Aikido, there are no enemies. The mistake is to begin to think that budo [the way of the warrior] means to have an opponent or enemy; somebody you want to be stronger than, someone you want to throw down. In true budo there is no enemy or opponent. True budo is to become one with the universe.*[39]

*Morihei Ueshiba*

## PUTTING IT ALL TOGETHER

Let's look at some examples of everyday conflicts and see how the Aiki Approach can work in a systematic and concrete fashion.

First, as we learned in Chapters 4 and 5, we can choose to respond to the conflict from a centered and connected place. This results in an essential rapport between the disputants. This is vital, because it results in a reduction, if not the total elimination, of the negative emotions between the parties, which in turn supports the disputants in getting in touch with a crucial question: Are they committed to resolving this conflict in a way that is mutually supportive? This is a critical point, because unless both parties are committed, the interaction will most likely be painfully long. There are many instances in life, from divorce to international conflict, in which one side sees value in continuing the conflict. This usually occurs when there is a great perceived power-disparity, and a low interest in supporting the needs of the other side or in developing a good, long-term working relationship. Both sides recognize that if an all-out fight resulted, the power imbalance would provide one of them with all the "spoils of victory."

In most instances, however, deeper examination of their interconnectedness will reveal to both sides the narrow limits of this short-term gain and the greater loss they suffer by continuing to fight. When both parties examine in detail the pros and cons of continuing the fight, they can see that the stress, struggle, and sense of separateness involved go against their deepest vision in life. The Aiki Approach is a powerful tool for resolving conflict because it helps disputing parties discover their common purpose.

The Aiki Approach will be most effective if the disputing parties are willing to sit down and discuss the issue. A neutral third party can be very useful to facilitate this. A facilitator skilled in centering and the process of conflict resolution can aid both parties in coming to an understanding they are unable to reach on their own.

The environment and the structure of a meeting also contribute to centeredness and rapport. An uncluttered, healthy environment promotes clarity of thinking. The room should be conducive to cheerfulness, peace, and understanding. Even the chairs should be arranged to promote working together rather than confrontation, angled in the same direction or placed in a circle rather than directly facing each other. Mix the two groups so as not to create separate camps. At the 1985 U.S.–USSR Summit Conference in Geneva, Mr. Gorbachev and President Reagan took a very important step in establishing rapport and a centered environment when they had their private "fireside chat."

Suppose there is a conflict between employer and employees over the creation of an employee lounge. With a commitment to resolve the conflict, management and employees can discover the true interests, feelings, and beliefs of each side.

| SUBJECT OF CONFLICT | POSITION | |
| --- | --- | --- |
| | Employer | Employees |
| Creation of an employee lounge. | We do not need an employee lounge. | We need an employee lounge. |

### INTERESTS, BELIEFS, FEELINGS

| Employer | Employees |
| --- | --- |
| I want to run my company in the most economical way and a lounge will cost money. | We work better when we're happy and when we feel management cares about us. |
| Employees should concentrate on their jobs. | A comfortable place to relax will make our work time more productive. |
| If I give the employees a little, they will just demand more. | If they can afford a new executive suite, they can afford an employee lounge. |
| Employees need more, not less, discipline. | If management trusts us and supports us, we will be able to make more of a contribution to the success of the company. |
| I feel taken advantage of. | I feel unsupported and unacknowledged. |

Similarities begin to appear as management and employees move further from their position or point of view on the lounge to a larger vision of what each party indeed wants. There is often a tendency to keep coming back to the initial positions on the issue and to return to a reactive evaluation of the other side. A continued checking of center, connectedness, and rapport is needed to support purposeful moving from the initial position to interests, beliefs, feelings, and finally visions.

It is very important that each side allow the other to express itself without interruption. A powerful technique that enhances listening is to have each side restate what it hears from the other in terms acceptable to itself. This develops empathy and understanding and makes appreciation and acknowledgment possible. Restatement alone can dissipate much of the negative emotion surrounding the conflict. In many cases, to be heard is all that both sides really needed in the first place. If so, the conflict ends right there.

After this understanding has progressed, it is important to articulate the visions that each party has.

## VISIONS

| Employer | Employees |
| --- | --- |
| I want an efficient working environment. | I want a peaceful working environment, conducive to doing my best job for the company. |
| I want my employees to be responsible and productive. | I want to be responsible and productive and to be perceived that way by management. |
| I want to feel good about myself as an employer. | I want to feel good about myself as an employee. |
| I want to run an optimally successful company. | I want to grow personally as well as make a contribution to a successful company. |

At this point, management and employees are in an excellent position to identify similarities in their personal visions and to cocreate a common vision. I have found it effective to have each party write out what they think would be a common vision and then compare them. Next, they should integrate them into one statement of consensus. A sample common vision in this example might be:

## COMMON VISION

We are a successful company whose individual participants contribute their full value to the company and receive appreciation, trust, support, and fulfillment in return.

Power arises when both parties participate in the cocreation process because they both begin to share (or be committed to) the common vision. Knowing that they have the same goal in mind, they are able to proceed together to cocreate solutions in which a lounge is not a conflict. And when both sides participate in cocreating solutions, they both become more responsible for carrying out those solutions. In a boss-employee conflict or a parent-child situation, there is often a distinct power difference. There is a tendency for the more powerful side, usually the boss or the parent, to dominate the solution. To the extent that this happens, the other party is likely to accept the solution passively but resentfully and is therefore more likely to give it up at the first opportune moment. Because they feel powerless, they often begin to grumble, criticize, or complain. When they cocreate the solution, however, they will be able to take more responsibility for its implementation.

Once a common vision is identified, then the focus can be placed on solutions rather than differences. Differences become much smaller in the light of a big common vision, and possible solutions can then be enumerated. While developing the solution, constantly ask the question, "If we were living this vision today, what would we be doing that would prevent us from having this issue arise as a point of conflict?" Whatever the solution(s), it is most efficiently and effectively determined through a process of cocreation.

## POSSIBLE SOLUTIONS

Management would agree to allot a percentage of future net profits for the lounge as an incentive for employees.

A temporary lounge could be established immediately as an indication of good faith toward the employees' expression of their needs and concerns.

In the late seventies, in what could have become a classically ruinous confrontation between labor and management, the Teamsters struck Anaheim Citrus, a small California company that processes citrus peels. The president of the company wanted more productivity, the truck drivers wanted more money. It looked like a no-win situation.

William Farley, the Chicago-based entrepreneur who had recently purchased Anaheim Citrus, flew out to California to mediate the dispute. A firm believer in cocreational principles ("Creativity and performance should be rewarded at all levels" and "Our people should work together in an atmosphere of trust and collaboration" are two of his managerial guidelines), Farley listened to both sides and came up with a proposal that satisfied both. He offered to pay the drivers by the load rather than the hour. Management would be off their backs and they could work as hard and make as much as they wanted. This potentially disastrous strike was settled in three days, to everyone's advantage. Management was guaranteed an acceptable level of productivity and the drivers were given the opportunity to exercise their own initiative and creativity in delivering the goods.

A typical opportunity for using the Aiki Approach in a family setting is the conflict created when a parent asks a child to do a chore such as washing the windows.

| SUBJECT OF CONFLICT | POSITION | |
| --- | --- | --- |
| | Parent | Child |
| Child washing the windows. | I want my child to wash the windows today. | I don't want to wash the windows today. |

| INTERESTS, BELIEFS, AND FEELINGS | |
| --- | --- |
| Parent | Child |
| I'd like to see my child learn some responsibility. | This isn't really my house. It's your house. |
| This family is a community and everybody should help out. | I have more important things to do. |

| | |
|---|---|
| My child needs some discipline. | I feel controlled when you make me do things. |
| I would appreciate some help with the housework. | This job is too hard for me to do well. |
| I want to be a good parent. | I want to be a good child. |

## VISIONS

| Parent | Child |
|---|---|
| I want my child to be responsible so he can live a happy, productive life. | I want to be able to take care of myself and to be happy. |
| I want to feel good about myself as a parent. | I want to feel good about myself. |
| I want a happy child. | I want happy parents. |

## COMMON VISION

We both are happy and responsible and we feel good about ourselves.

## POSSIBLE SOLUTIONS

Child doesn't have to clean the windows, but instead chooses another equally significant chore for practicing discipline and responsibility.

Child selects his own schedule and hours for doing the windows. If the child successfully demonstrates his ability to do a good job without constant reminders, then he will be given more freedom in other areas, such as staying up later.

Once the solutions are decided, it is advisable that both parties verbally declare their commitment to the solution and then spend some time envisioning the future.

If Joe and Betty Baggodonuts and their son Billy recognize their common vision of a comfortable and enjoyable home, Billy may decide that he will do his part by being responsible for mowing the lawn. If Billy commits to doing the lawn on Saturdays, it would be valuable to examine future scenarios before they actually occur.

Questions that lead into this might be:

"Well, Billy, if something comes up next Saturday, like a big beach party, what will we do?"

Or,

"Billy, if I find that the lawn didn't get cut one week, what should I do as your Dad?"

This gives Billy the chance to reply, to create his own discipline.

Or together, parent and child might ask the question, "Next year at this time, if we've really worked together on keeping agreements, what will our relationship be like?"

By envisioning the future, by having both parent and child, or employer and employee, as the case may be, imagine the next day or month or even year and think up as many considerations or situations as possible that would test the solution, they are testing their commitment to the solution. This process works to insure that future stumbling blocks become stepping stones to a deeper, more conscious commitment to their relationship and the realization of their common goals.

*Anyone can count the seeds in an apple.*
*No one can count the apples in a seed.*

Anonymous

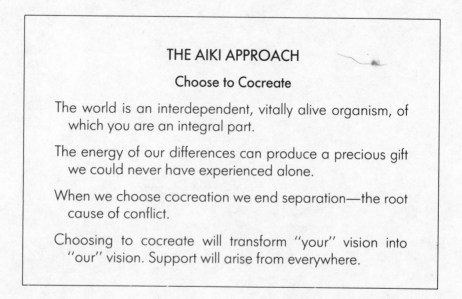

## THE AIKI APPROACH

### Choose to Cocreate

The world is an interdependent, vitally alive organism, of which you are an integral part.

The energy of our differences can produce a precious gift we could never have experienced alone.

When we choose cocreation we end separation—the root cause of conflict.

Choosing to cocreate will transform "your" vision into "our" vision. Support will arise from everywhere.

# FIGHT, FLEE, OR FLOW

"Come to the edge of the cliff," he said
"We're afraid," they said
"Come to the edge of the cliff," he said
"We're afraid," they said
"Come to the edge of the cliff," he said
They came.
He pushed.
They flew.
Guillaume Appollinaire

# 10. Don't Sweat the Small Stuff

The caveman walked through the forest and suddenly froze. The extraordinary quiet all around him was not new to his experience. Birds no longer chirped, and there was no rustle of leaves or twigs from animals scurrying about. Immediately all the cells in his body became hyperalert, ready to move quickly and powerfully in any direction. The heat of built-up energy found a release in small drops of perspiration on his hands and forehead. He was ready—seeing, smelling, listening acutely for the signal to move. He might slowly retrack his steps with all senses alert or break into a high-speed retreat. Or he might be in for the fight of his life, with every muscle and fiber in him exploding with the instinct to survive—to do or die.

Naturally and effectively, our caveman's nervous system sent messages to his endocrine system, which produced all the hormones he needed to fight or flee. In moments of crisis, our biological systems can transform us into superpeople. Our endocrine system, through the teamwork of the hypothalamus, pituitary glands, and adrenal glands, stimulates our heart to supply greater oxygen and glucose to every muscle in the body. Our respiration rate goes up to give us greater endurance, our blood-clotting ability increases to handle a potential injury, our eyes dilate to increase our visual ability, and our kidneys hold more water and sodium so that our blood volume expands. We are supercharged.

All of this is a gift that psychophysiologist Hans Selye calls the General Adaptation Syndrome, or GAS. It is a gift derived from over fourteen hundred known physiochemical reactions that are activated within seconds in our bodies in response to stress.

Stress is simply pressure on the human being. Conflict *is* stressful. Remember, we define conflict as *an interference pattern of energies*. When two energies of different intensities and directions come together, there is increased pressure. It is our response to this pressure of conflict that holds the trump card, dictating whether this stress is harmful or useful. Selye called the potentially damaging aspect *distress* and the potentially beneficial one *eustress*.

Stress in humans can be clinically defined as a *psychophysiological abnormality at the structural or chemical level caused by undue pressure of experience*. Among all that mumbo jumbo are the key words *undue pressure*. What is undue for one person may be a piece of cake for another. For a professional football player, waiting to catch a kickoff before eighty thousand spectators may not cause undue pressure, but speaking in front of a national television audience may. It's easy for me to speak in front of large groups, but please don't ask me to sing solo around the campfire.

Our modern-day caveman, Joe Baggodonuts, leaves his luxurious, electronically-vibrant-and-wired-for-speed dwelling and proceeds to move through a concrete jungle at high rates of speed. He is encapsulated in plastic and metal, held tightly in a seated position that allows for none of the brisk physical movements of his walking ancestor. He, too, discovers a sudden stillness in his jungle. The car in front of him is moving at fifteen miles per hour in a thirty-five-mile-per-hour zone. He glances at his watch and notices that he will be late for an important meeting if he continues at this rate. The pressure builds. The biological gift of fourteen hundred psychochemical reactions that he inherited from his cave-dwelling ancestor starts to flow. His forehead perspires, his hands sweat, he grips the wheel tighter in an attempt to release some of that superenergy that's running through his veins.

By this point in a conflict, his caveman ancestor had already fled or fought, venting this power. Our modern-day friend considers his options for releasing the energy. He can leap out of the car and sprint down the middle of the highway, screaming his lungs out. Or he can wait until the car in front actually stops, and attack it with all his physical strength, biting fenders, kicking doors, and pounding windshields. Fortunately he is still sane enough to see this as inappropriate. He curses under his breath, and frets and worries about being late. The physical releasing of all this energy is suppressed. His anger and upset build. He allows the energy to partially vent itself as he honks his horn, raises his fist, and yells through the windshield.

The ridiculousness and ineffectiveness of his response is evident. *Here I am yelling at somebody's grandmother because I think she is ruining my life. I must be a very sick man.* Any stress that was vented returns even stronger now, with feelings of guilt and powerlessness. Meanwhile, all of those new fight-or-flight chemicals are still floating around in the bloodstream with no place to go. And they accumulate with each daily, seemingly insignificant conflict—when Joe forgets someone's name, misplaces his coat, or waits up at night for his teenager. Distress becomes a constant companion.

The daily piling up of distress is one of the chief factors in degenerative illnesses, which run the gamut from chronic headaches to cancer. Is there any hope for our modern-day hero?

There are proven ways to treat effectively the symptoms of distress and to mitigate their cumulative buildup within the mind and body. These ways fall into basic categories: diet and nutrition, exercise, managing thoughts and relationships, and rest and relaxation. Just as we are under stress periodically throughout the day, we can adopt daily programs in each of these areas to dissolve that stress.

It is the doing of the program, not the worrying about it, that will make the difference. It's no wonder that the players in the game, who are on the field releasing their adrenaline, are exhausted but relaxed after it is over, while the coach is the one looking for some medicine to handle his ulcer.

In previous chapters, we have learned to turn the stress of conflict into an ally. We know that we can deal with stress at its source rather than just react symptomatically or inappropriately to its pressure.

When we treat conflict as a dance, the pressure makes for a useful dancing partner rather than a distress producer.

Distress in humans is caused by how we respond to the conflict between "the way it is" and "the way we want it to be." If we perceive the difference as some insurmountable gap or chasm we are incapable of crossing, or believe we are held back by people or events beyond our influence, the struggle and suffering begin. We are inviting stress to take a seat, usually right on top of us.

Is it possible to live a life of such power and integrity that stress never manifests itself in a destructive form? Can we take responsibility for the source of all our experiences so that the pressures of life are just opportunities to enhance our creativity and productivity in accomplishing our true purpose?

To live a life of such power we must dissolve this gap between where we are and where we want to be. Instead of focusing on the gap, the key is to focus on building a bridge. The bridge is simply constructed from the clarity of your vision. It is knowing that you can have what you really want in your life, right now, prior to "doing" anything.

## CLARITY OF VISION

How clear is your vision? Can you taste it, touch it, hear it, and see it so vividly that your very cells vibrate with it? If you begin to do this, magic will occur. For years prior to winning the gold medal in the 1976 Olympics, Bruce Jenner visualized himself winning all the events in the decathlon. Jack Nicklaus never hits a golf shot without an exact picture of it in his mind. Then he physically lets himself be an instant replay of that picture. Lee Evans, the 1968 gold medalist in the 400 meters, visualized each second of his race so clearly that he saw every stride he would take.

If you are going to use the power of visualization, it is important first to discern your true purpose. The closer you get to your deepest desire and *raison d'être*, the more natural and powerful will be your visualization. One of the best ways I know to become increasingly clear about my real purpose for being on this planet is to come up with an important goal in my life that I can declare in a specific and measurable way. Then I ask the simple yet provocative question, "If I obtained this goal, what would I get?" When I am able to answer this, then I repeat the question with the new result, and so on, until I get to the essence of what I really want.[40]

A typical example is the following conversation that I had with a sixteen-year-old boy:

"What do you want, Bobby?"

"I want a sports car." (No problem here in getting him to be specific and not ambiguously abstract or philosophical. I've found that kids are good at being concrete.) He proceeded to describe it perfectly, right down to the color of the upholstery and the make of the sound system.

"Let's say you had that sports car. What would you get by having it?"

"Well, I'd get more friends."

"Ah, I see. What you really want is more friends. And if you had more friends, Bobby, what would you get from that?"

"Let's see. Well, to tell you the truth, if I had more friends . . . well, what I'd really get is Natalie to like me."

"Ah. What you really want is Natalie to like you. So if you had Natalie liking you, what would you get from that?"

At this point, of course, Bobby turns slightly red and looks at me, knowing that we both know what he's talking about.

I smiled, understanding him.

"Well, Bobby, let's say you got that. What would you really get from all that?"

A more contemplative look took hold of Bobby. "Well, if I got that, really had Natalie liking me, I guess what I'd get is . . . I'd get to feel OK, like I'm somebody."

"So, what you really want is to be somebody. If you were somebody, what would you get?"

Bobby wondered how long this was going to continue, although he was at the same time very interested.

"I think what I'd get, if I were somebody, is I'd get to feel good about myself. That's it. I'd start to really like myself and know that I was OK."

Now, at this point I could tell by the change in his mannerism that we were getting near to the heart of his vision. "So, what you really want, Bobby, is to know that you're OK, to like yourself, to love yourself?"

The response from Bobby needed no verbal statement.

"Let me ask you this, Bobby. If you had all this love for yourself, all this respect for yourself, what would you do with it all? Would you just sit there with it all, puffed up like a balloon?"

Bobby thought for a few seconds before replying. "No, if I really loved myself, I'd be able to give it to others. I'd just share it with others. I'd just be happy and be able to create happiness around me."

At that point, I noticed that Bobby was actually feeling that way inside by the way he spoke, by the way he stood, by the gleam in his eye, by his smile. I knew we had gotten to his vision, his vision of really wanting to give to others, to love others, to give the love he felt for himself. Now, there's a *vision*.

What's interesting about this vision is that it took a rigorous questioning process to get to it. But in the process of getting to it, something beautiful emerged. The specific form of his desire (i.e., the car) took a backseat, and we discovered what he really wanted was a quality of being that was outside of form.

Having explored this exercise with hundreds of different people, I have noticed that the outcome of the exploration is always similar. We move from a specific form or want into knowing what we're really after is a quality of being that is outside of form, that is formless. Inevitably it is not just to *get* something—love, understanding, respect, support. Instead, it's more than that. It's always making a contribution that's wanted—giving love, being understanding, respecting others, and serving those who need us. Our true vision becomes a verb—to love, to serve, to understand.

And even more exciting, when you are clear about your vision and recognize it is a quality that is outside of form, you begin to realize you can have that quality of being *right now*. What an eye-opener for Bobby. I could see his shoulders straighten, the energy flow in him, his new centeredness—that positive, confident, powerful attitude that he took on as he declared, "Yes, what I want is to be loved and to give love to others."

Of course, the question from him shortly after was, "Well, does that mean that I don't have to get this car to get all that?"

I looked at him intently and asked, "What do you think, Bobby?"

He said, "Well, it's obvious. I don't."

There is beauty and power in understanding that your vision is a quality of being that you can choose to have right now.

You can still proceed toward specific outcomes such as a car, but this time, as you proceed, you do so from a prior place of fulfillment, of centeredness and completeness. Your struggling becomes joyful movement. You let go of the distressful aspects of bridging some great gap between an unhappy you and a happy you. You are not dependent on some form called a sports car or house or relationship or title, or any other of those gold medals for which we are constantly striving all our lives.

The power in discerning with great clarity your purpose in life is that it then vibrates within every cell of your body. The gap between where you are and where you want to be dissolves. Instead of engaging in frenetic, anxious activity to reach distant goals, you allow your directions and outcomes to emerge from that centered place of your vision. You integrate within your mind/body/spirit all those wonderful feelings and qualities of being you think you will receive from the gold medals, but *prior* to achieving them. The frustration and feeling of inadequacy is replaced by the fruit of your vision *now*, in the present. The energy and power needed to achieve success is naturally there because you have already moved *beyond* it. When you choose to live your vision in the present moment, the actual movement toward some form—a job, a sports car, a relationship, or making a difference on the planet—becomes full of joy, awareness, and appreciation.

People who are living their vision create inspiration for us all. They can be found in any form, from trash collectors to housewives to presidents. One of the great influences in my life was a man who spent most of his life cooking and washing pots and pans. Whenever I entered his kitchen, Brother Bernard would inevitably be there, scrubbing a large pot. He would look up with a big smile and twinkle.

"Hi, Tom. Great day, isn't it?"

What I always wanted to do at that moment was to grab the nearest Brillo pad and start in beside him. That old Zen saying became a real-life expression for me: "Before enlightenment, chop wood and carry water. After enlightenment, chop wood and carry water." It wasn't just pots Brother Bernard was scrubbing. He was scrubbing the dirt and distortion from his perceptions of the universe, creating a sparkle in his very soul. My own scrubbing suddenly had a new purpose. In his book *Zen Flesh, Zen Bones,* Paul Reps tells an old Zen story.

----

*Ryoken, a Zen master, lived the simplest kind of life in a little hut at the foot of a mountain. One evening a thief visited the hut, only to discover there was nothing in it to steal.*

*Ryoken returned and caught him. "You may have come a long way to visit me," he told the prowler, "and you should not return empty-handed. Please take my clothes as a gift."*

*The thief was bewildered. He took the clothes and slunk away.*

*Ryoken sat naked, watching the moon. "Poor fellow," he mused. "I wish I could give him this beautiful moon."*

----

We may ask, once we have our vision, why do we do anything? Once the stress is gone, where is the motivation to act? The answer, as usual, is all around us. If you look at nature and the universe, you discover the inherent principle of continuous creative movement and evolution. An oak tree doesn't stop once it has produced an acorn or two. It keeps on growing, making living fibers out of air, sunlight, minerals, and water, becoming more magnificently itself.

Living from your vision works the same way. Your mind and body expand to accommodate and express your vision. Right now, the expression of Bobby's vision may look like having a neat car and being with Natalie. Later it may expand to include a home, a family, a career, creating a world that works for everyone. As he grows, his vision will become deeper and richer.

Look at the truly powerful, those such as Buddha and Christ, who appear from time to time and make such a difference on the planet. The quality of their vision and of their being is such that we regard them as divine. They are already living beyond any success that we may be dreaming of. Yet it is this very state that moves them to act powerfully and effectively to share their reality with the rest of us. At any moment, they already have everything they want or need to have —a deep place of knowing that they are living their vision now. What may appear to us as a great struggle to achieve some divine good is simply the moment-by-moment expression of what is already alive within them. They are living examples of that of which they speak. Once again the choice is ours: to live in distress or in the light of our vision.

When your vision is crystal clear, taking action happens naturally. Larry Bird doesn't write notes reminding himself to practice shooting a basketball. His self-image is that of a great ball-player. So he naturally does what a great ball-player does, which, of course, is to practice. Arnold Palmer does not forget his golf clubs nor John Denver his guitar. Their tools of action have become an integral part of their lives, like eating or sleeping.

When you are in touch with your true purpose and it is vivid and alive within you, *now*, the necessary actions to accomplish it appear as if by magic. Vietnam veteran Jon Scruggs wanted to show his appreciation and love for his friends who had died in Vietnam. He had no political or financial clout. All he had was a vision of service and the clarity of a way to express it. His first action was simple—tell others. Within a few years, all the necessary resources gathered around him. The Vietnam War Memorial Fund was created and today the memorial is a reality.

Little Sarah Kreinberg of Portland, Oregon, was only seven years old and suffered from an inoperable brain tumor. Her vision was much greater than just her own illness. She saw herself as a help to others who were suffering. Emptying her piggy bank of five dollars and donating it to the Ethiopian relief fund was only a start for this very determined, very caring child. The answer on how to act further came immediately. After seeing a newspaper photograph of a starving Ethiopian baby and learning that a local bank was matching funds for famine relief, she really went to work. By making and selling Christmas ornaments, she earned $6,500 in one year for her Ethiopian brothers and sisters. And all this in the same year that she underwent a series of chemotherapy treatments and four operations to relieve pressure on her brain.[41]

Apparently no one told these people they didn't have the necessary power or influence to make a difference and that they had their own personal stress and conflict to worry about. Their vision was deep and clear, and they acted on the vision enthusiastically, joyfully, and effectively. Their personal problems and stress paled in significance to the task at hand. The best rules I ever heard for handling stress are these three:

---

1. Don't sweat the small stuff.
2. It's all small stuff.
3. Since it usually doesn't work to fight and it doesn't usually work to flee,

*flow.*

---

Have you ever noticed that when you are committed to your deep vision, most of your daily stress and conflicts become just small stuff? Your "stuff" doesn't get in the way of who you really are and where you are really going.

Rick Little had lots of difficulties in his life while growing up. Instead of playing the powerless victim, becoming more distressed over the pressure he was under, he began to wonder why school, which took up most of his time, rarely dealt with the real-life problems all teenagers face when growing up. He decided to do a study of what teenagers really needed to learn and, as a result, designed a course called "Skills of Living" or the Quest Curriculum. Do you think he would have done this if his personal vision was that of an insignificant kid who is constantly being neglected and whose goal is to get back at everyone? Do you think that creating this major breakthrough in our educational system did anything to dissolve some of his stress and build any personal power and responsibility in this nineteen-year-old? His vision of service to himself and to all school children was so vivid that his actions "flowed" regardless of the many conflicts in his path. His proposal to create the curriculum was turned down by 150 foundations before the Kellogg Foundation agreed to do it. When the Kellogg spokesperson also turned down his $55,000 request, Rick thanked him, prepared to go on to the next foundation.

The official said as Rick was leaving, "We've turned down your $55,000 request because it is not enough. We want to give you $130,000." Rick Little did not sweat the small stuff. He just continued flowing from a centered place of vision.

*. . . everytime you think you are not happy, say "I am happy." Say it strongly to yourself, even if your feelings are contradictory. Remember, it is your self-image and not you. Just as fast as a fish can move in water, you can instantly change to a happy, balanced attitude.*

Tarthang Tulku Rinpoche
"The Self-Image"

# 11. No Boundaries

When the stress of conflict emerges in your life, what do you do—fight, flee, or flow? Some people who have been working with the Aiki Approach immediately respond by declaring righteously, "I flow, of course!" This is usually a good indication that they have misinterpreted the Aiki Approach and put boundaries on the meaning of "flow."

There is nothing inherently wrong with establishing boundaries. Without boundaries of some sort we couldn't drive our cars safely down the street, carry on a conversation, or focus our minds. Problems arise when we unconsciously allow our boundaries to determine our identity—how we think, feel, and act.

Issues arising around sex, race, and culture are an obvious example. There is no question that we do have physical and psychological differences in those areas. It is when we allow these boundaries to determine our understanding of another person that we get into trouble. We are then being guided only by our past rather than by discovering the person anew, without all of our filters. If we still considered the Great Wall of China to be the barrier and symbol of separation it was originally designed to be, it would create an automatic reaction when we saw it. Yet in today's world, to consider the Great Wall as an actual physical deterrent would be absurd. When we give up the past imagery, we discover a symbol of commitment and artistry, esthetically weaving an awesome perspective of human history, connecting thousands of miles with thousands of years.

When our lives are run by the forms and images of our past experience, we may find ourselves in conflict with the living, breathing reality before us. The use of old, inappropriate forms of response in a new or changing relationship can only lead to distress. It also is limiting. To avoid the feeling of distress, we tend to identify with the people who are most like ourselves. Friendship extends only to those who agree with us.

The basis of the Aiki Approach is to establish an identity with the real center of our being, which is all-embracing and infinitely adaptable to our own needs and the needs of others.

Let's consider the geometry used by the founder of aikido, Morihei Ueshiba, as symbolically representative of man, and see how we can use it to expand our own possibilities.

As you can see, the above symbol is an integration of three shapes: a triangle, a circle, and a square. As we described in Chapter 7, these shapes help us to understand the complexity of conflicts and our choices about how we can respond to them.

The triangle represents those responses that have a particular focused movement, such as direct resistance to the attack or moving in a specific manner away from the attack (disengaging or avoidance).

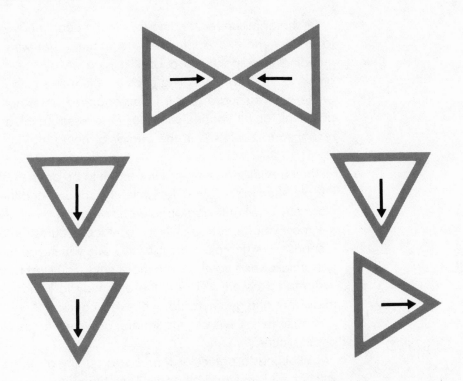

In contrast, the circle represents a flowing, rolling, or blending response, such as is often found in negotiation, collaboration, and acceptance. The square indicates a lessened ability to move dynamically and symbolizes the response of holding a position, or doing nothing (passive disengagement). It may also represent passive resistance.

Each person has a tendency, in crisis or conflict, to operate from one form more than the others. Which is your tendency?

Primarily a triangle, directed and possibly combative

Primarily a square, consistent and possibly resistant

Primarily a circle, agreeable and possibly indecisive

A major misunderstanding that many people have as they begin to explore the Aiki Approach is to assume that what I am recommending in response to a conflict is to always be the circle—the blending, flowing, accepting choice—thumbing your nose at the triangle or the square. But it is important to note that we have the potential for all shapes within us. The essence of an appropriate response to conflict is in the quality of being, not in any particular form.

In the Aiki Approach, it is important to be open to all possibilities. People often misconstrue the circle, the square, and the triangle as a hierarchy of what is appropriate and what isn't, with the circle being the most appropriate. But when you lock yourself into one form of response, the domain of possibilities with which you have to operate gets smaller and you become more rigid. You start to create a belief system that asserts, "This is the only way to handle it." You try to throw that one geometric form at every conflict.

The truth is, the circle, the square, and the triangle all have appropriate places.

Aiki is not a particular form but a quality of being that includes within it all forms and all possibilities to create peace. Our ability to include all possibilities extends our capacity for compassion, empathy, and understanding. When we feel that only certain forms are appropriate and all others are wrong, we set limits and boundaries on our understanding. Without understanding, we cannot respond appropriately. Understanding and the flexibility to respond in many different ways will support us in finding the approach most appropriate to the situation and will inevitably expand our power in handling conflict. A good illustration of this is the story of a "tough cop" who arrested a very angry man:

------

When I had to take him to a paddy wagon, he spit in my face—that was something—and he went after me with a chair. We handcuffed him and put him in the truck. Well, on the way, I just had to get past this picture of things, and again I affirmed to myself, "This guy and I are brothers in love." When I got to the station, I was moved spontaneously to say, "Look, if I've done anything to offend you, I apologize." The paddy wagon driver looked at me as if I was totally nuts.

The next day I had to take him from where he'd been housed overnight to criminal court. When I picked him up, I thought, "Well, if you trust this vision, you're not going to have to handcuff him." And I didn't. We got to a spot in the middle of the corridor which was the place where he'd have jumped me if he had that intention. And he stopped suddenly. So did I. Then he said, "You know, I thought about what you said yesterday, and I want to apologize." I just felt this deep appreciation.

Turned out on his rap sheet he'd done a lot of time in Michigan and had trouble with guards in jail. I symbolized something. And I saw that turn around, saw a kind of healing, I believe.

So what really happens if you're going to explore whether or not this vision of our nature really has power? Maybe people will say you're taking chances. But you're taking chances without any vision; your vision is your protection. Maybe they'll say you're sentimentalizing people. But it's not about people. It's about principle and truth. It's about how the universe is. Maybe they'll think it's idealistic; things could never be this way. Well, for me, things are this way already; it's just up to us to know that more clearly.

I see that my work is to hold to an image of who we all truly are, and to be guided by that. And I have been guided by that. To greater strength and security . . . within myself and on the street.[42]

---

Building upon aikidoist/author Terry Dobson's work,[43] I use an exercise that supports us in understanding and including *all* the possible responses to conflict—particularly the ethically questionable ones of physically fighting back, withdrawing, or doing nothing. The key is to develop a personal mental scenario in which those forms are an appropriate response.

For instance, I was at St. Benedict's, a Trappist monastery in Colorado, leading a workshop on conflict resolution. I asked the monks to give me all the appropriate responses they could think of for resolving conflict. I stated that I would write them on the board only if they were unanimous selections. Unconditional love, acceptance, negotiation, and mediation came out quickly and easily with no negative reactions. I drew a large circle around those responses, indicating the flowing, blending nature of them.

I then suggested a couple of different responses to conflict. "Well, how about doing nothing? Can we justify that?" And I drew a square to symbolize that response.

"Sounds like not taking responsibility," one monk said. "I can't allow that to go on the board."

"If we are not accustomed to exploring lots of possibilities," I replied, "and if we are locked into forms—one is right, one is wrong—we often become locked into judgment. We would exclude some forms entirely and not have empathy when another person uses them. So instead of excluding the whole generic form, let's explore possible scenarios to see if there is one in which doing nothing is appropriate."

"Sometimes," a monk suggested, "when a person is upset and ranting and raving, it is best to calmly do nothing until he settles down and you can find out exactly what he is upset with."

"Ah," I said, "there's a scenario that works for you. Does that work for everyone?" And as they proceeded, each in his own mind, to develop at least one scenario in which doing nothing would work for them, we were able to include it as an appropriate possibility.

We proceeded to go through more responses, some of them very interesting to discuss in a monastic setting, such as physically fighting back (or actually harming a person) and using deception or diversion.

The monks found deception very difficult to accept. "It sounds like lying, or cheating, or not having integrity," one monk said. I asked for a specific scenario that would allow them to expand their minds, to include rather than judge. Another monk stood and said, "Imagine you were limited in your ability to move—your legs paralyzed—and your child was crawling on hands and knees on a wet floor toward a light socket. You had a ball that you were playing with in your hand and you began to bounce the ball on the floor. The child, as he was heading toward the light socket, heard the sound, noticed the joy with which you were playing with the ball, and turned and looked, and then looked back at the light socket and made a choice. He changed his direction and started heading for the ball."

Playing with the ball was, in this case, a deception or diversion, but the activity worked exceptionally well given the situation and the playful quality of children. The monks accepted this scenario.

The responses of fighting back or doing physical harm to a person met with great resistance. I drew a triangle on the board with the words *fighting back* in the middle. There was an almost unanimous reply that fighting back and doing harm to a person were always inappropriate. The only dissenting voice came from the abbot of the monastery, Father Michael, who raised his hand and to the surprise of everyone replied, "Yes, I can see that." He spoke about a number of social justice problems in history, the black and white problem and several political revolutions, in which he could see that the most appropriate method was to fight back. Many of the monks still disagreed. I stated that it was very important that we develop a specific scenario in which we could empathize with the "fighting back" choice. I suggested one.

"Imagine that you are paralyzed in a wheelchair and cannot speak and have the use of only one hand. Sitting across the room from you is your three-year-old, playing. In rushes the mad ax-murderer, with his ax up, ready to cut, within inches of coming down on your child. The only thing you have in your hand is a .357 Magnum." My question to the monks was a simple one. "Get very real about this situation, and tell me, would you or would you not pull the trigger? And if you could not pull the trigger, can you change the scenario in some way, shape, or form which would put you in a position in which you could pull the trigger?" Eventually they were able to include fighting back as an appropriate response in certain extreme situations. As we let go of the boundaries around what is a correct form and what isn't, our mind expands to include everything and our potential to respond appropriately becomes limitless. And because we have so many options, we can make clear decisions on such difficult issues as fighting back. You may come to the conclusion that you would never physically or mentally harm someone unless there was *no* other alternative and innocent life was endangered.

Remember, it isn't just the particular response that makes the difference. It is the quality of your being. Consider a person who's operating as a circle, as a blending and accepting person. If she is centered, her being is whole, even, and flowing and looks like this:

If she is uncentered, her being is like an unbalanced tire.

Instead of blending, flowing, and being harmonious, she becomes wishy-washy, scatterbrained, indecisive. Her responses are inappropriate and, like the unbalanced tire, she wears herself down in the process. The quality of her being is not the same.

The centered triangle is committed, strong, and forceful in a positive way. The uncentered triangle is angry, aggressive, manipulative, and stressful.

A person who responds as a centered square is likely to be stable, consistent, and firm. An uncentered person operating out of this form is often authoritarian, dogmatic, and self-righteous.

Have you ever watched any of those John Wayne movies in which, when the crisis comes, he straps on his guns and proceeds to blow away the enemy with great gusto and courage? It's a very satisfying release and, in the context of the movie, appropriate. The Duke is standing at the center of his universe, creating order and justice.

Real life is rarely, if ever, so one-sided, and our attempts to fit every conflict into the neat formula of a strict competition between good and evil rarely succeed. After getting all pumped up with your image of the Duke, you go into the office and see a colleague with whom you are having trouble. You strap on your metaphorical guns and challenge him to a shootout, only to feel later, whether you won or lost, uncomfortable and remorseful. Why was that response appropriate for John Wayne and not for you? Is it because you're not right enough and tough enough to play that strong, macho role?

The truth is, it's simply a matter of how much you value the relationship. In war, there is no center, no common vision, only a very high consideration for your needs and your community's needs and a very low consideration for the needs of the "bad guys." When our uncentered minds are full of warlike competitiveness, fighting back appears to be the only choice.

When centered, we feel all the aspects of our relationships, not just the unresolved conflicts, and have a much stronger commitment to the quality of our interactions. So even after enjoying John Wayne, you can walk into your office and know that you have a greater need to create a strong working relationship with your colleagues than the Duke has with his enemies. Such a high consideration for the needs of all parties requires cocreation and collaboration, not fighting and win-lose competition. And this usually requires considerably more creativity and courage than throwing a right hook, pulling a trigger, or pressing a button. The courage to cocreate and collaborate is what it takes to be truly human.

In a life full of quality relationships and activities, we don't necessarily give the same values to every interaction. Different responses may be appropriate. If you are in the midst of writing an important report and a salesman calls to talk to you about an electric ear-cleaner, you may simply choose to *avoid* the situation and tell him you are busy. If a dinner date wants to eat Japanese food and you want to have barbecued chicken, but neither of you feels that strongly about the issue, *compromise* may work best and you may end up happily dining on chicken chow mein. Or you may have very little desire to choose a movie, while your partner has a strong need to see a particular one. Then, simple *acceptance or accommodation* may be appropriate.

In any particular issue, an awareness of the relationship between the strength of your needs *and* the strength of another's will guide you in determining an appropriate response. Whatever your response, it needs to emerge from a centered, loving place to be effective. Although the form of a response to conflict is indeed important, it is the quality of being behind the form that can make all the difference.

No matter how incorrect or upsetting someone's action may be to you, the key to resolution is to continue acknowledging your relationship with that person. Neem Karoli Baba, an Indian guru, put it very simply. "Do what you will, but never put anyone out of your heart." A mother can point a finger at her child and scold him angrily for running into a busy street, but if her response comes from a place of love, the form may be appropriate. On the other hand, if the same anger, intensity, or rage comes from dislike or hatred of the child, the communication is altogether different. It becomes a form of abuse. Vince Lombardi, the famous football coach, once said, "You don't have to like what your players do. But you have to *love them*."

# A LESSON IN COMPASSION

The importance of being able to include all forms of response as possibilities within your own mind provides you with a foundation for empathy, compassion, and forgiveness. When you are able to expand your mind to include everything, you operate from full potential. You have no boundaries on your ability to understand and to love others.

*Years ago there was a Christian monastery in Egypt. It was very poor materially. The only precious possessions were the Scriptures, written on three beautiful scrolls, that were always left open on a table in a small study near the chapel.*

*One day a monk came out of the study, screaming, "Father! Father! Someone is stealing the scrolls!"*

*The abbot of the monastery came running to the study and saw that two scrolls were indeed missing. But on the window sill was the third scroll. It had been dropped by the thief.*

*The abbot grabbed the third scroll and dashed off in the direction of the fleeing thief. After a long chase, the abbot finally caught him.*

*The exhausted thief collapsed on the ground and surrendered himself to his captor and awaited the subsequent severe punishment rendered to thieves in those days.*

*Instead, the abbot stood in front of the man and handed him the third scroll, exclaiming, "I have been chasing you for quite a while. I wanted to give you this third scroll. You forgot to take it and it is the most important one. The teachings would be incomplete without it."*

*With this, the abbot bowed and walked back to the monastery.*

*Shortly thereafter, the thief returned to the monastery with the scrolls, totally committed to becoming one of its monks.*

As we integrate the Aiki Approach into our daily lives—increasing the depth of our awareness and heightening the sense of our connectedness—we become committed to having quality relationships. We begin to understand that all people are operating out of one of two modes: fear or love. Actions that are injurious or create disharmony and distress result from fear—from a contracted mind that is limited in its ability to see alternatives. In the alienation of fear, people, no matter how repulsive their actions, are crying out for help to resolve their insecurity and separation. When we understand this, we can let go of our judgments about their actions, show them compassion, and support them in creating the love they are looking for. As they learn to operate from a place of centered love and fulfillment, their actions will be more appropriate and beneficial to all. However far from this place they may appear to be, we always have the choice to open the door of love or to lock ourselves in, in fearful competition.

The willingness to spend time and energy to collaborate and co-create emerges as we recognize this: Powerful relationships are our *choice*.

Pope John Paul demonstrated this power when he entered the jail cell of Agca, the gunman who had attempted to assassinate him in 1984. He had gone to the jail to forgive the gunman. The Pope recognized that all human possibilities lay within both of them, and that there was no final barrier between himself and the assassin. From this compassionate understanding, he was able to choose love rather than separation, and to offer it to the man who had tried to end his life.

When you are able to accept and include within your own mind all the possible responses to conflict, you naturally give birth to the gift of compassion.

## Please Call Me by My True Names

Do not say that I'll depart
tomorrow because even today I still
arrive.

Look at me; I arrive in every second
to be a bud on a Spring branch, to
be a tiny bird, whose wings are still
fragile, learning to sing in my new
nest, to be a caterpillar in the heart
of a flower, to be a jewel hiding
itself in a stone.

I still arrive, in order to laugh and
to cry, in order to fear and to hope.
The rhythm of my heart is the birth
and death of all that are alive.

I am the mayfly metamorphosing
on the surface of the river. I am
also the grass-snake, who,
approaching in silence, feeds itself
on the frog.

I am the child in Uganda, all skin
and bones, my legs as thin as
bamboo sticks.

I am also the merchant of arms,
selling deadly weapons to Uganda.

I am the 12-year-old girl, refugee on
a small boat, who throws herself
into the ocean after being raped by
a sea pirate.

I am also the pirate, my heart not
yet capable of seeing and loving.

I am a member of the politburo,
with plenty of power in my hands.

I am also the man who has to pay
his "debt of blood" to my people,
dying slowly in a forced labor
camp.

My joy is like Spring, so warm it
makes flowers bloom in all walks
of life.

My pain is like a river of tears—so
full it fills up all the four oceans.

Please call me by my true names so
that I can hear at the same time all
my cries and my laughs, so that I
can see that my joy and pain are
but one.

Please call me by my true names so
that I can become awake, so that
the door of my heart be left open,
the door of Compassion.

Thicht Nhat Hanh

*What we see, and like to see, is cure and change. But what we do see and do not want to see is care, the participation in the pain, solidarity in suffering, the sharing in the experience of brokenness. And still, cure without care is as dehumanizing as a gift given with a cold heart.*

Henri Nouwen

---

## THE AIKI APPROACH

### No Boundaries

In Aiki, there are no boundaries. You become open to all possibilities.

In Aiki, no possible response is automatically ruled out or in.

Discovering the appropriate response requires opening your mind and your heart.

Opening to others leads to compassion and forgiveness.

The response that arises from the centered, inclusive state will be the most beneficial one possible.

# TAKING IT
# TO THE STREETS

# 12. Putting It to Work

Over the last five years, I have been receiving letters and phone calls from people who have used the principles of Aiki to produce remarkable changes in their daily life. There appear to be no limits to the applicability of this approach, except those self-imposed by the practitioner. The stories that follow represent a wide variety of personalities and professions. Yet in each story, we can discover the principles of the Aiki Approach in action.

## I.

My buddy and I were skiing high above the treeline near Aspen, Colorado. It was still snowing lightly when we set out from our camp at Conundrum Hot Springs, but the desire to ski foot-and-a-half-deep fresh powder had led us up to the top of the vast, untracked Alpine bowl.

Just as we turned around to begin our descent, a heavy cloud rolled in, enveloping us in a whiteout so thick we could barely see each other, although we were just a few yards apart. All shadows disappeared and the boundary between ground and air became invisible. The only way to sense the ground was to feel it through our boots and skis; we were skiing in a white blindness.

We had chosen an area free of cliffs, rocks, and avalanche runs, so we were in no objective danger, and as long as we kept going downhill we would eventually end up back in camp.

Still, there we were at thirteen thousand feet, skiing down a mountainside through soft, heavy snow on flimsy cross-country skis—a tricky proposition in the best of lighting.

We let ourselves go, feeling our slippery, twisting, cockeyed way down the mountain. All bets were off—this was a brand new, uncontrollable situation in which all our carefully practiced turns were of no avail. There was nothing left to do *but* center—center the body over the skis and respond to the feelings of speed and direction coming in through the skis, feet, legs, into center, and then out through the torso, head, and arms that were flailing around, trying to keep up with all the surprises that the ground produced. Center. Nothing to do but center, bring it all back to center and start over again, moment by moment, turn by turn. Fear and frustration dissolved into awareness. Falling was just part of the process. We had no goal other than to be there, enjoying this extraordinary situation.

We emerged from that cloud after a half hour of exhilarating self-discovery. Unplanning, unpatterning our mental control over our bodies, getting out of the way and letting the natural feedback mechanism take over. "Yes, yes . . . no, no, yes . . . no, no, no, . . . yes, yes!" My internal dialogue was reduced to the simplest terms, allowing the experience to possess fully my mind and body.

Breaking out of the mist and into a grove of widely scattered spruce, I finally discovered something to do with my eyes. From my center I projected a thin, red beam of energy along the perfect line I wanted to ski and let my body go again. Following that "imaginary" line, I skied the most perfectly enjoyable and flowing run of my life. As I write this I wonder: Could I have projected that *ki* energy in the whiteout, used my *ki* to set my course down the mountainside, without my eyes to stabilize it against the background? I don't know. I'll just have to go out there again to find out.

*Mountain Guide*

## II.

In our community the generation gap is not a problem; it is one of our greatest resources. The "gap" is mostly artificial anyway, the result of segregating people according to their ages and societal functions—students, producers, and retirees. Rather than making these differences into boundaries, we have used our school system to take advantage of all that young people and senior citizens can offer each other.

In the elementary schools, the seniors are invited to drop in for a cup of coffee and use the hallways for exercise during the winter months. Before you know it, the seniors are right into the swing of things, kidding with the students, sitting in on classes, swapping stories and adventures and sharing skills. Instead of isolating kids behind hallowed walls, the place becomes a community, and everyone is enlivened.

Middle school students volunteer to serve lunch to the nursing home folks, read stories, and chat. The seniors respond through the Foster Grandparent program or share their skills and experience as classroom consultants.

At the high school level, the students sponsor the annual "Spring Fling," a senior citizen "prom." The theme, music, and decorations are developed in a series of joint meetings. The music may not always be in tune, but the students and seniors sure are.

*Superintendent of Schools*

## III.

My wife and I once had our early morning meditations punctuated daily by the sound of an automobile horn announcing to our neighbor that his ride to work had arrived. I was increasingly irritated by this and one day said to my wife, "If I had powers, I'd give that guy four flat tires."

"That," said my wife, "is why you don't have powers."

Her remark moved me to serious contemplation, and a few days later I announced, "If I had powers, all I'd really do is bust his horn."

"That's a bit better," she said.

Further serious contemplation. One morning I declared, "I've got it! If I had powers, I'd see that his horn didn't work in this neighborhood."

"That's a bit better yet," she said.

I was now quite puzzled, because I thought I had finally discovered the "right action."

At last I realized, "If I had powers, I wouldn't be distracted by that horn."

"Yes," said my wife.

*Musician and Writer*

# IV.

I travel worldwide to meetings and workshops having to do with whales. Over the years two major conflicts have managed to sharply polarize many people who are interested in whales. One issue is whaling and the other is holding whales in captivity in zoos and aquariums. The Aiki Approach has given me the freedom and insight not to choose sides but to try to understand both parties and then to find a creative way to resolve the conflict.

Representing the Windstar Foundation as an observer at the International Whaling Commission meetings for the past three years, I've gotten to know both whalers and conservationists. At first the whalers were quite hostile. One Norwegian refused even to shake my hand, expecting me to call him names and try to talk him out of his livelihood. The next year, though, I went right up to him and we began talking about him and his family, staying off the subject of whaling. We became friendly and he introduced me to the rest of the Norwegian delegation. In turn, I introduced them to some of the conservationists whom I knew were reasonable and wanting to get all the facts. Aiki gave me the courage to take this human approach rather than to move to one side or the other. It really paid off for me.

One of the most rewarding experiences I had at the IWC was bringing together an elder of the Eskimo whaling community and a conservationist, both of whom were concerned with the beluga whale. At this time the conservationist was looking for the way to most effectively safeguard the beluga's habitat. The Eskimo was very interested and asked the conservationist many questions. Then he began telling us all the little things he had learned about the beluga from his many years of living with them and hunting them. Their mutual respect for the animal was obvious, and they parted with a pledge to share their knowledge and energies.

Little things can make a big difference. An amusing thing happened at one meeting where I took the initiative to move the chairs a little closer together, so that the Russians, Japanese, and Americans were almost literally rubbing elbows. A Russian and American were sitting next to each other. Both were chain-smokers and neither was able to smoke during the sessions. Their common discomfort created a bond, and they began smoking and talking together during the breaks.

Similar understandings can also come about between the zoo and aquarium professionals and the anti-captivity groups. Here again, many of the people involved have become so polarized that they have never actually sat down face to face and talked. Both groups want to educate the people of the world about how wonderful and special whales are. Both groups want to end the destruction of the animals' habitat and both groups are interested in preserving the species. What a place to start! By bringing together a conservationist who is particularly good at doing informational graphics on whales and an aquarium official who needed some graphics-updating in his facility, I was able to ease the tension between them and pave the way for a new relationship. In this way, the rightness or wrongness of their positions was subordinate to their common goal to educate the public. The animals we all love so much will be the benefactors.

*Environmentalist*

## V.

I was marching in one of the umpteen sixties demonstrations. We were at the Presidio in San Francisco and I was right up there in front. There was a huge line of flak-suited men. Helmets. Clubs. Eyeless eyes.

On the "other" side, we were clothed in self-righteousness and screeching slogans, chirping insults. It's great to know you are absolutely right and "they" are absolutely wrong.

All at once, the men, in unison, swung their clubs around their heads and charged. They were beating anyone they caught and they were heading straight for me. I turned around. In back of me there was a man with a guitar, sitting on the ground and singing a song to his dog. I thought of running. Instead, I sat down with that troubadour and started petting the dog. Chaos and screaming all around. The police ran right around us as if we were invisible. For all I know, at this moment we were invisible.

If I had run, I would have landed in a hospital, jail, or both. I chose a different relationship at the crisis point. By instinct.

*Social Activist*

# VI.

I had recently been elected president of our city's chamber of commerce. An acquaintance of mine who was the president of a small manufacturing company was not a chamber member. One evening at my house, he congratulated me on my election, so I asked him if he would be interested in joining. He declined, saying, "I don't see what the chamber has to offer me and I don't really want to put my time into that kind of thing."

Before I had seen Tom's film on conflict resolution, I immediately would have jumped on the defensive and gone through my laundry list of programs that the chamber has to offer and their benefits. Instead, I let his reaction go on by.

"That's fine. By the way, how is business?"

"Well, quite frankly, I'm faced with a real dilemma," he said. "We're getting a lot of competition from overseas, and we've got to decide whether to shift our manufacturing to either Japan or Taiwan and lay off about half our work force here, or to slug it out where we are, knowing that there is a real possibility we'll be out of business in a couple of years. It's a tough decision to make."

I asked him if he thought anyone else in town had ever faced a situation like that. I told him I knew some of the larger companies (Kodak, Hewlett Packard) had gone through the same thing recently and asked him if they might have some insight for him. "Maybe they could," he said, brightening up.

"One of the things we're going to do this year is start a council of manufacturers who get together two or three times a year to discuss their common problems. One of the topics we plan to cover is foreign competition," I told him.

"How can I get involved in that?" he asked. "I'd even be interested in putting something like this together. Do I have to be a member of the chamber to do it?"

"Well, it would help," I replied.

"Then we'll join."

The key to this naturally successful outcome was getting myself on *his* side and finding out what was going on in *his* world.

*President of a Real Estate Company*

# VII.

I always thought when there was trouble, fights between people, you either had to call the police if it were potentially dangerous, or go to court. Going to court seemed the only way to really resolve it. That is until you went there. Then you realize you've spent all this money and time and, even if you win, you're more stressed out afterward. The concepts of Aiki changed my whole attitude about what is possible, but I wasn't sure if they would work in the inner city where I live.

I moved to San Francisco recently and I can't believe what I'm seeing. A couple of friends of mine who live in a crowded little neighborhood were literally at war over a barking dog problem with their neighbor. It wasn't just name-calling, but also threats of violence to each other. Actually if you live in a big city you know that this is typical stuff. Most of the violence and trouble that happens in tightly packed cities comes from just that kind of problem, over parking, loud noise, trash, broken love affairs, family disputes. These are the things that really keep the cops on their toes. Anyway, instead of letting this thing go on to cops or courts, they decide to go to something called Community Boards.[44] This isn't some government operation, but instead it's made up of volunteers from the neighborhood. So I tag along and we find ourselves in a comfortable little room having tea or coffee with the "enemy," the guy they were ready to kill the day before. What follows is a simple process facilitated by a couple of the volunteers in which each side lets out their grievances and their feelings. And there were some ugly things said, believe me. What was really amazing was that the other side doesn't interrupt but really listens and afterward restates the complaints against them.

Man! I've never seen this in a courtroom. Just by venting their emotion and being heard, you can feel the hostility dissolve and relationships build. They may not like each other, but they're not so willing to knock the other guy's head off anymore. After all the "stuff" came out, some calmness seemed to settle in, and pretty soon they were bringing up solutions. The "enemy" agreed to come over and get acquainted with the dogs and their owners, while the owners agreed to keep closer tabs on the dogs and to encourage him to telephone if they were bothering him. The actual solutions weren't nearly as important as the remarkable change in the relationship that occurred between the disputants. And the resolution seemed far more solid than any courtroom decision.

And now it's going on in our schools! Kids, mind you, not teachers, have their own organization for handling disputes. They go around in orange shirts with a big "Conflict Manager" written on it. And these aren't just the "goody two-shoes" types, but the tough kids as well. They use a similar process but of course in their own fourth or fifth grade jargon. And it works. At recess, two boys will be fighting over a ball and two kids wearing orange shirts come over, smile, and ask, "Would you like to resolve this thing?" And they do. It's amazing. Those kids are taking hold of their lives now and learning vital skills at such a young age. I can't wait to see what the world will be like when these kids are running things.

And I hear they're even taking this attitude of peacemaking home. Can you imagine a couple quarreling and their ten-year-old walking over calmly and saying, "Would you two like to resolve this thing? I think I can help."

*Inner-city Dweller*

# VIII.

I was just another pretty face looking for a party when my motorcycle caught fire, burning me over 35 percent of my body. I learned very quickly that I was going to need to see the world differently and to come up with some new strategies about how to deal with life. I was very fortunate to believe that there really is no absolute relationship between any two variables. You can be funny-looking and be quite successful and quite happy, quite pleased with yourself. Conversely, there are people running around who seem to be perfect yet are living in *mental* wheelchairs. I understood that it was my up and my down, and that I was in charge of driving my own spaceship. I didn't spend an inordinate amount of time being depressed and wondering why my cup was half empty. I could see that the cup was still half full. I didn't have to worry any longer about whether I was the most handsome guy at the party. I could get on to more important things.

People would stop and stare. I would certainly get their attention. Instead of sitting there waiting for their sympathy, I would turn it around by giving them an opportunity to see how they could win from getting to know me, how they could turn setbacks in their own lives into victories.

Four years later, I became paralyzed in a plane crash. Now I had to deal with a limitation that was even more severe than the burns. I was fortunate enough to realize that before I was paralyzed there were ten thousand things I could do and now there were nine thousand. So I could either spend the rest of my life dwelling on the one thousand that I lost or I could focus on the nine thousand that were left. By focusing on the nine thousand, I have so far been able to do only a few—become a mayor, a successful businessman, and a talk show host. The reality is that if you do only four hundred or more of these things in your life, you're a Bucky Fuller or an Albert Einstein.

I could have let my burns and my paralyzed body be walls of confinement. But instead I have found that they are wonderful opportunities which open the door to deeper values and to the joy of being alive on this planet. Sure, there are days when I watch longingly as other people walk or jog up mountains. But then, I have found other ways to get to the top.

*Politician and Entrepreneur*

*Man is most nearly himself when he achieves the seriousness of a child at play.*
Heraclitus

# 13. Masters of Aiki

When I look back, I see that kids have been my greatest teachers. They are masters of living in the present, creating magic out of the ordinary, and making play a viable way of being in the world. Having three children has provided me with quality instruction. When my children were infants, they taught me about how play brings us into the present. When I come into the house, all scattered and upset and concerned, there is Ali with a big smile, right there, not thinking about next week or about what happened that morning. Right here—now! When Ali needs something, she lets me know, vocally or physically, right away. When she doesn't want something, she pushes it away. She comes from her heart all the time. You can't help but be pulled into the present when you're with a little child.

When I'm with Ali, I've also noticed that when my mind wanders, when I'm occupied with the future or the past, she becomes increasingly irritable with me. She's totally aware that I'm not present. If I'm playing with Ali, and I am right there with her—she's crawling, I'm crawling, she's playing with a toy, I'm playing with the toy—she'll continue. Yet when my mind is no longer there and I'm only going through the motions of playing, who am I fooling? Not Ali. She lets

231

me know that right away, by banging the toy on my head or by using another similarly effective means to express her opinion about my inability to reside in the present. I couldn't ask for a better teacher.

When children are learning to walk, they never see themselves as failing and succeeding, failing and succeeding. When a child moves from point A to point B, he does it in a pattern that looks like up—down; up—down; up—down. On a graph, the pattern looks much like dolphins swimming. And the toddler's playful, joyful attitude is just as strong in the down times as it is in the up times. Adults, on the other hand, when learning much simpler tasks (very few are as difficult as tasks that children are learning), often go through a pattern that looks more like fail, succeed, fail, succeed, fail, fail, and quit.

Adults often *try* to learn how to concentrate. A child is a master of concentration. No trying is involved. Have you ever watched an infant focus on a speck of dust or a piece of dirt or a particle of food on the floor? She'll stare at it; she'll be concerned with it; she'll touch it, pick it up, put it in her mouth. She is totally consumed. She doesn't miss any of it. She'll hold it out at arm's length, pull it up close, wave it, hand it to somebody. Her attention is right there with it. There is no separation, really, between what she sees and who she is. She is in the present, discovering. Her world is her.

In fact, if you look at the six conditions of the Aiki Approach that allow us to move beyond success, you will see that those are the natural conditions from which all infants operate.

Young children are *centered.* Have you ever looked at them? They sit so straight. Their posture is in perfect alignment. They're full of *ki.* Their arms feel like they're puffed up. They don't sag. If you hold a child up in the air, his whole body is held like a pumped-up balloon, full of energy. All his limbs are full of *ki.*

Children are *connected,* and not just within their bodies. They don't see themselves as separate from the world. Everything they see and touch is part of them.

They are fascinated by the world around them. It's all magic. They don't just have a discovering attitude, they *are discovery.*

These young Aiki masters are seeking to *understand;* they are always open and looking to figure things out. They are interested in everything.

And being *flexible* and willing to *change*? There are very few times when infants aren't totally willing to give up whatever it is they are consumed by in favor of something else. For infants, whatever comes in front of their eyes is worthy of their appreciation, worthy of adapting to, worthy of scrutiny. We carry infants around from place to place—they're wide-eyed and willing to go. They're open. Physically, they are extremely flexible, sucking their toes, getting into one pretzel position after another.

And they are willing to *cocreate*, to create any kind of fantasy, to change their reality. That's the way a child looks at you. They don't just look at your physical body. They look all around you as if they're checking out your energy field, your *ki* sphere. A small child sitting at the dinner table reaches over and with ease lifts a bottle of milk that weighs a quarter of what he weighs. It's not physical strength. It's *ki* and intention. They are uninhibited, expressing themselves with a powerful sense of self-esteem.

If you want to learn a lesson of forgiveness, watch young children. A child will come into the house extremely upset with someone, exclaiming, "I hate him! I never want to see him again! I'll never play with him again!" And within two minutes, all is forgiven. He is outside in the sandbox, playing with the child he was upset with as if nothing had happened. And nothing did, in his reality. Everything has been totally forgotten and forgiven, and he is with the other child fully in the present, not carrying any ill thoughts or regrets.

When I look further at children, I come across a startling revelation: I was one once. We all were. And when I ask the question, "What day, what hour, what minute did I leave the child and become the adult?" I realize I can't answer. The truth is, we have never lost the child. The child is always right there. The child is alive when we give ourselves permission to be completely in the present, to live lightly and simply.

Children are the best models of the Aiki Approach in action. It's a blessing that every village, every country, every neighborhood, and many homes have within them a master teacher to support us in moving beyond success—a very small child. May they teach us to reopen the door to the child within ourselves.

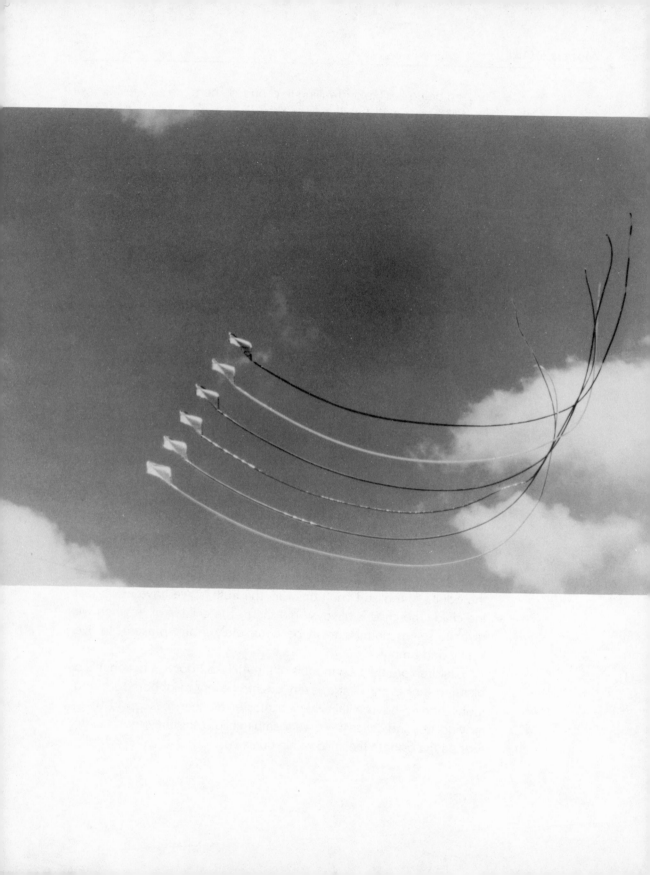

# EPILOGUE
## Beyond the Gold

*Unless we change our direction, we are likely to end up where we are headed.*
Old Chinese Proverb

The purpose of this book is to remind us to move through life with power *and* grace. It's about choosing to come to the center of any storm, receiving the energy of your life without judgment, and using that energy with a smile of gratitude for the possibility of a new twist or two of creativity. To live Aiki is to let the energy of life in, to let it surge through your body, straightening your back and recharging your being. It is to breathe, eat, speak, and act with dignity and with elegance and with a deep bonding to the earth upon which you walk. We are pearls, however gritty and rough we sometimes appear to be. The conflicts and pressures of our lives are the sandpaper necessary to smooth out these rough edges.

This epilogue is written because I know that when we truly embrace ourselves, we can't help but embrace the world. Embracing the whole world, accepting all its pain and beauty, is not "saving the world" with a display of arrogance or righteous anger. It is reaching out with love and power to the world, as a natural expression of the light and vision that we have within.

235

Throughout this book we have been making new connections, discovering the power of centeredness for creating freedom and harmony in our daily lives and thought. Where does it all lead? What about the magnitude of today's world conflicts? Are they also opportunities for significant growth and change on a global scale? Could it be that humanity is taking a massive evolutionary step toward greater global connectedness?

It has been shown by such noted scientists as Jonas Salk that all species go through a crisis point of evolution in which they move toward a more interdependent harmonious relationship with their environment. This shift is what insures their survival. This balance between population growth and resources has been described by author-scientist Bob Samples as a process of dynamic equilibrium.[45] This "evolutionary centering" is nature's way of moving us from separateness to connectedness.

The gift of being human is that we are able to consciously participate in this evolutionary shift. Instead of seeing the human drive to climb ever higher as inherently flawed and stressful, we can recognize it as simply evolution's way to nudge us into an expanded relationship with the world around us. The urge to constantly climb and struggle simply for personal gain takes on less significance as we get in touch with the joyous process of connecting ourselves to those around us.

When our sphere of identity is contracted to include only our personal or family needs, we tend to treat the rest of the world as a series of opponents. The idea of service to the world appears as a chore, a burden, a method of alleviating guilt, or a way to acquire ego strokes. However, as we continually expand our sphere of identity to include others, we begin to experience a quality of fulfillment that heightens every time we give value to other people's lives. We begin to know the *joy* of service and to somehow sense that every time we add value to the lives of others, we are also adding value to our own. Ironically, giving becomes a self-serving act, as we find it impossible to distinguish where we end and where the outside world begins.

Over the years, I've had the opportunity to work with people from a wide variety of fields: sports, business, and entertainment. Many of these people were among the most successful in their fields. And in many cases, they were struggling with just this question: "Where do I go now that I've reached the top? Is there anything worth living for beyond the gold?" These questions were of vital importance to them as individuals. They also address our situation in the world as a whole. Following the Aiki Approach we discover that the answers to our individual and collective problems are intimately and joyfully connected.

A few years back, I had the good fortune to work briefly with Muhammad Ali, the world heavyweight boxing champion of the sixties and seventies. During the afternoon we spent together, I saw a different person than the one I had perceived through the media. I found a big, warm teddy bear with a magical child inside. After only a brief conversation, he opened up in a very heartfelt manner.

"Look at me. I'm forty-two years old. I'm tired, fat, and feel very old. It's even hard to get out of bed in the morning. Look at this face. It was the most well-known in the entire world. I would receive the best VIP treatment in any nation in the world and meet with any world leader of my choice. I literally had the applause of nearly four billion people. I think I feel lousy now because I don't know what to do for an encore."

I could see that he had fallen into one of the most difficult traps of all—the lethargy and depression that can come from having been on the top and noticing that everywhere else seems low in comparison.

I replied to his tough question with a tough answer.

"When you've had such success, there probably is *no* encore that will do it for you—as long as you have a limited model of what success is. There is only a remote possibility that you can duplicate the kind of personal adulation you received as world heavyweight champion. Yet within this great dilemma is a magnificent opportunity. You are finally forced to play an entirely different game. You need to choose a bigger ring than you could have ever imagined the young Muhammad Ali climbing into. The only truly acceptable encore now is for you to let go of your individual need for recognition and take on a bigger need, the support of a most important team—Team Earth. A deep sense of fulfillment emerges within us when we contribute real value to our planet and to the people around us. And what better model could the whole world have than a world champion transforming the big, strong arms he used to beat people up into the even bigger and stronger arms necessary to support and to hug others? Getting out of bed will become easy. Getting to bed will become the new and better problem."

At that moment, I could see the light sparkle in the champ's eyes. His entire posture changed, and the magic of the young Ali emerged as he enthusiastically began to talk of a dream he had long held.

"I've always wanted to use my fame and recognition to help bring about world peace. I'd like to join children, who I love deeply, in getting world leaders to connect all nations in peace."

As he leaped up to shadowbox the effectiveness of such a mission, he looked years younger. The fluid movements, the quick mind, and the charismatic power of a man of passion returned and filled every cell in his body. The crisp banter and showmanship of the past were vividly alive again. But this time, the match was even more exciting to watch because I felt he was "boxing" for all of us.

The opportunity to go beyond success is not for superstars alone. It is available to each of us. It is not just a matter of dreaming. It is acting on those dreams. It is having the courage and commitment to participate 100 percent as a member of the human family in creating a truly sustainable future for our children. It is participating in the creation of a world in which all people have food, shelter, and love, and the opportunity to become all that they can be. It is choosing to plug ourselves into the main circuit. An infinite supply of juice and joy becomes available.

*We train in hopes of being of some use, however small our role may be, in the task of bringing peace to mankind around the world.*

                                                                        Morihei Ueshiba

Making this universal connection is what the Aiki Approach is ultimately about. Throughout this book, we have been practicing ways to resolve conflicts and live without boundaries. Let's look at the whole world from this Aiki perspective.

We are all living together on one planet in the Milky Way Galaxy. This living, breathing, interdependent organism that holds all of us is cruising at 66,000 miles an hour, eight hundred times faster than a speeding bullet, each and every day of our human history. We have traveled together, in spite of our differences, 580 million miles this year alone.

In this book we have explored the difference between unconscious reaction and conscious response. We have learned that we have a choice during crises. In Chapter 8, we explored those choices in depth. We can react by contracting into fear and separation or by expanding out to growth and creativity.

In our personal conflicts, the ability to choose may be more apparent than in world crises, where the magnitude of difficulty and complexity appears overwhelming. Seen in this light, we can understand the common tendency to withdraw from these conflicts with feelings of insignificance and powerlessness. As we withdraw, we increase our isolation and separateness. When we isolate ourselves, we limit that which is available to us. As we create limitations, we begin to perceive our resources as scarce.

When we get stuck on the perception of scarcity we spend excess time on defending what we have. Our fear and alienation toward others increases as we perceive them taking from our "fair share." Despair over this situation often leads to inaction and the numb acceptance of fate. Rage, on the other hand, leads to blind action (such as conquest) that may satisfy immediate needs but does not creatively address the issue of long term sustenance.

While playing on a hot summer day, two young children notice a dripping garden hose. The drop-by-drop trickle provides them with a desire for a real thirst-quenching gulp. But as they grab the hose from one another they feel the lack of real fulfillment. They spend all their time bickering and fighting over the little drops rather than using their creativity to follow the hose to its source and turn on the faucet. If one does discover the faucet, because they are so small it may take both of them to turn on the valve. If they've spent enough time fighting, they may be so alienated from one another that the thought of working together never occurs to them.

This sounds like a case of simple early-childhood foolishness and lack of understanding. Could it be that adults and nations have similar problems? It seems that only after great pain and struggle are we willing to let go of our obsession with self-preservation and let life flow a little. The world of scarcity and struggle that we imagine for ourselves becomes a self-fulfilling reality.

A formal statement of this scarcity consciousness was made by Thomas Malthus in his 1798 essay, "On Population":

---

Population, when unchecked, increases geometrically. Food and agriculture increase only arithmetically. Therefore, there is not enough to go around at this time and this situation has existed for all of human history.

---

Even though Malthus's numbers give an accurate view of the conflict between the rates of growth in population and agricultural capability, he failed to understand that we are able to respond to such conflicts with choice and creativity. He was right about the geometrical expansion of population. It took all of human history until the year 1800 for us to reach a population of one billion. One hundred years later we were approximately two billion. Fifty years later we reached three billion and twenty-five years later, in 1975, we reached four billion. By the summer of 1986 we were a total of five billion.

But Malthus's theory breaks down in the face of humanity's capacity for innovation and technological advance. This ability has allowed us to produce more than enough food to go around. Conditions such as hunger strengthen our belief in scarcity, when, in fact, scarcity is not the problem. According to the United Nations' Food and Agriculture Organization's 1986 statistics, we produce enough food for every person to have 2.5 pounds of food per day. There is enough grain alone for everyone to have two loaves of bread each day. Scarcity is *not* the problem. Hunger may be a distribution, cooperation, and sociopolitical problem, but it is not a scarcity problem.

And yet to this day, we humans still hold this finite, closed perspective that there *is not* and *will not be* enough food or other supplies on our "Spaceship Earth" to go around. We earthlings have accepted this scarcity belief as if it were some divinely ordained principle. We have taken every instance of scarcity as "proof" that this is the way it must be in all aspects of life. This attitude may be an important clue to understanding why the human family as a whole is not living abundantly today. This, of course, leads us to Charles Darwin, who said:

". . . Therefore, only the fittest will survive."

By applying this to all human affairs, we have reinforced the scarcity myth with the concept of competition at all levels of life, believing that somebody always has to lose. We all recognize the healthy, positive aspects of competition in sports and even in some business situations. But what I'm talking about is the tendency to play a win/lose game in all areas of living, from family relationships to international politics. And yet our evolutionary nature has provided us with the consciousness and capability to choose centeredness and abundance. We have the capacity to choose balance between population, resources, and environment, to shift from the win/lose paradigm to one of cooperation and expansion.

Without this perspective, we humans continue to unconditionally accept the scarcity concept in areas as critical as those of water, food, and energy. Is it any wonder that great tensions and separation emerge when there is a disparity in consumption? For instance, Europe, the USSR, and the USA combined (one-fifth of the world's population) consume two-fifths of the world's food and three-fourths of the world's energy production.[46] Those figures might make some lesser-developed nations upset, wouldn't you think?

Our belief in scarcity is strengthened when we use primarily nonrenewable resources. Energy, like food, is often misunderstood. Virtually all of the energy we are now using comes from our earth's savings account—biomass, such as wood, and nonrenewable fossil fuels and uranium—to the detriment of our environment and to the increased tension between nations. Yet at the present time, all our energy needs make up only 1/600,000th of 1 percent of the daily input to us from the sun. In addition, energy-saving technologies already developed, such as new kinds of lights, motors, and appliances, allow us to use energy more efficiently and economically each year. The U.S. alone saved over $150 billion between 1973 and 1985 in this manner. If the U.S. continues in this fashion, it is estimated that up to 1 trillion dollars in energy will be saved by the year 2000.[47] When we choose a more connected relationship with our environment in this way, we discover that energy is not scarce. A sustainable future with sufficient energy is possible.

What does seem to be scarce is our willingness to consciously change our direction and thinking *before* a crisis hits. Competition over supposedly scarce energy creates international tensions and insecurity and fuels the arms race. Amory and Hunter Lovins and the Rocky Mountain Institute have spearheaded an important change in thinking about national security by providing an entire new range of choices. For example, the Institute statistics reveal:

> If our American homes were energy efficient, it would displace foreign oil and become a security alternative to the Rapid Deployment Force, which is designed to secure our access to Mideast oil fields. In fact, one year's budget of the Rapid Deployment Force, put into energy efficiency programs, could eliminate our Mideast oil imports. Quadruple efficiency light bulbs are safer and cheaper than nuclear power plants. Instead of bending our foreign policy and our morals around a need for chromium, we could take advantage of the revolution in materials science, and use advanced substitutes. Technologies to make third world agriculture sustainable and more productive can reduce North-South tensions. And wise energy use can reduce the threat $CO_2$ poses to our atmosphere.[48]

Evolutionary thinkers like Bucky Fuller have been able to show the inaccuracy of the scarcity myth. One of Bucky's main points was that humans have a commendable tendency to do more with less. We can apply this tendency to do more with less to every aspect of our daily living. We used to communicate with Europe via a 175,000-ton transatlantic cable. We now do it far more clearly and efficiently with a one-quarter-ton communications satellite. We took two years to circumnavigate the globe in Magellan's time. One hundred years ago, a steamship could complete the journey in two months. In the early days of aviation, it took two weeks. Today it takes two days. The space shuttle gets around in two hours. And with telecommunications, we can connect anywhere, live! In areas as diverse as communications, transportation, building, and manufacturing, we have proven our ability to do more with less. Our future goals can include expanding our level of efficiency in areas such as food and energy. The scarcity myth continues to crumble as we understand more deeply how we are connected and use this knowledge to discover new ways to do more with less.

In today's world, inequities exist. It is when we perceive those differences as the inevitable result of scarcity that protecting resources becomes vitally important and a military buildup is seen as an absolute necessity.

---

Instead of supporting Japanese involvement in World War II, Master Morihei Ueshiba quietly retreated to a small farm. In founding Aikido years before, he had announced a new way for the warrior, a way out of war:

"As ai (harmony) is common with ai (love), I decided to name my unique budo 'aikido,' although the word aiki is an old one. The word which was used by the warriors in the past is fundamentally different from that of mine. Aiki is not a technique to fight with or defeat the enemy. It is the way to reconcile the world and make human beings one family."[49]

---

In any single day in 1986, we earthlings spent over $2 billion on making weapons to aim at our fellow crew members. If security is our goal, we must still ask the question, "Are we spending our money in the best possible way to achieve it?" If our vision is one of abundance and cocreation, should we deal with the need for security in a different manner?

When we respond to today's crises from the evolutionary perspective that conflict is the catalyst for us to make significant changes toward harmony and equilibrium, we begin to see our choices in a new way. Instead of contracting in an ever-tightening spiral of defensiveness, we expand in an ever-growing circle of cooperation and understanding. From this centered place we have the courage to embrace conflict knowing that it is a splendid opportunity to choose a future of growth and prosperity. Let's look at the present state of the world and its hidden opportunities.

At the Windstar Choices for the Future Symposium in June 1986, Peter Bourne,[50] president of Global Water, Inc., stated, "Immunization is another key to saving children, and while there is an international campaign to immunize every child against the six basic childhood diseases, this may well go down in history as the year in which we were willing to spend $900 billion on armaments but we were not willing to spend $1 billion to see that every child was immunized."

It is easy to be frightened or angered by such numbers, but when we look at every commitment of energy and money as a fresh opportunity to choose, the magnitude of our possibilities can become exciting, rather than depressing. Some more facts that may help us understand our present choices are:

- Worldwide military spending in 1985 was over $800 billion, while one person in three cannot read or write, and one in four is hungry.[51]
- 100 million people worldwide are employed directly or indirectly in military operations. That number is approximately three times the total number of teachers and doctors in the entire world.[52]
- Over a twenty-year period, all the money spent by international agricultural research centers was $629 million, or only 37 percent of the cost of one nuclear submarine.[53]
- Indira Gandhi, the late prime minister of India (where about 75 percent of the population devotes most of its waking hours to the sowing, cultivating, harvesting, and processing of food plants) observed in November 1981 that for the price of one nuclear submarine, it would be possible to:

    —plant 200 million trees, or
    —irrigate 1 million hectares, or
    —feed 50 million malnourished children in
        developing countries, or
    —buy 1 million tons of fertilizer, or
    —erect 1 million small bio-gas plants, or
    —build 65,000 health-care centers, or
    —build 340,000 primary schools.[54]

- In the approximately one minute it takes you to read this page, the world has spent $1.7 million on military activity.[55]

Throughout this book, we have seen how easy it is in our own lives to get lost in conflict to the extent that it becomes a matter of winning and being right rather than of obtaining our true vision. Is this what we are doing on an international level as well? As we continue to polarize around our differences, is it any wonder that the evening news plays back to us pictures of wars, drug problems, ill health, and crimes? The same old scenarios play over and over, to numb audiences—only the names change among the standard plots.

*Is this being human? Is this being all that we can be?*

Sometimes our problems are so large they become invisible. We close down, and when they appear in front of our faces on the evening news, we accept them as inevitable. When a child is about to run into a busy street of traffic, you take action. It's real, tangible. You know that it is unacceptable and you do something about it *now*. What would it be like if we took that same action toward the larger, immediate problems the world faces? What would we do if we responded to a deeper bond with each other and to the planet?

To support workshop participants in deepening their connection to the entire human family, I ask a hundred people to form a circle, each person representing 1 percent of the world's population, or fifty million people. I have them visualize the group as the entire human family. I ask eighty of these to bend over at the waist as if exhausted. They represent the 80 percent of the world without adequate shelter. Fifty people from the bowing group are then asked to get down on hands and knees. They represent those humans who do not have access to clean water or sanitation, half the people of the world.

Next, I have twenty of them lie flat on their stomachs, representing the 20 percent of our brothers and sisters suffering from abject poverty, hunger, loss of hope. Three people turn over, belly up, graphically representing the 3 percent who die each year of hunger. Lastly, I have ten of the people who are still standing raise their hands high over their heads, illustrating the approximately 10 percent of the world that controls 75 percent of our *recognized* resources.

The message gets across with few words. It takes courage to look at the world in this way. And yet in order to take appropriate action, it is important to "embrace the tiger." I ask the participants, "Right now, how are you responding to these ideas? Are you closing down to these images, feeling contracted or fearful? This reaction is understandable given the magnitude of the conflict and the depth to which you are connected. This may be an excellent moment to use the Aiki Approach to turn conflict into opportunity. How is your breathing? Get centered and take a deep full breath, filling your body with energy and power. When you exhale, release any sensations of pain, tension, or contraction that you may have. Changing the world always starts with your willingness to let go of anything that keeps you stuck, from fear and apathy to solidified belief systems. Since we are continually faced with such conflicts, this technology is extremely useful for preventing a return to old patterns of resisting or judging and for turning fear into the power of positive change. Whether your reactions feel 'good' or 'bad' to you, notice that they are simply your own and part of your overall response pattern to the world." As we choose to work on ourselves first, our ability to respond appropriately to the world will naturally expand.

The participants and spectators experience the dilemma we humans have created. As we stare at the crumpled choreography of human existence—bent over, kneeling, and sprawled out—they can't help asking, "Is this the best that humanity can be? Is this the world we would create if we truly operated as a member of one human family, crew members on a single spaceship?"

And how is the world community reacting to this family abuse? We spend even more money on weapons and defense to protect our "scarce" resources. And is there any evidence that we are buying any more security? It's as if we are flying on a major airline together and seven of us have hand grenades (representing the seven countries known to possess nuclear weapons) and everyone else has handguns. Pretty scary flight, isn't it? The feeling of scarcity gets even stronger as we continue our "you or me" game. And yet, within all this collective insanity, we find the greatest opportunity in human evolution: the chance to discover who we truly are. We have finally progressed so far in our technological ability to wage war that we have made war obsolete. The irony is, we just haven't realized it yet. It has happened so fast, that we have nothing to put in the place of a war machine that is obsolete and which creates ever greater instability. It's similar to the automotive industry continuing to build bigger and bigger cars for years because their factories were set up to do so, even though the demand and the times had changed and they were losing money.

The world community, by and large, knows that nuclear war is unwinnable and suicidal. We finally have a common problem/conflict around which the entire world can gather—a nuclear warhead. This touchable, visible, real-life object of death is an incredible opportunity. For the first time, we crew members of Spaceship Earth have encapsulated all our fears, vulnerabilities, and anxieties in one deadly form. The combined statement of the Soviet and American physicians who together received 1986 Nobel Peace Prize said it as powerfully as I've ever heard it said:

---

We will have one world, or we will have no world.
We will live together, or we will die together.

---

There has never been a better opportunity to discard the old rules of fear and scarcity and replace them with love and cooperation than right now. It is a magnificent time to bring out the good news!

The good news is encapsulated in the word *abundance*. As Buckminster Fuller said, when we dedicate our lives to livingry, rather than weaponry, we create a full bowl for all of us. When we know that there is enough, we are far more likely to accept and even appreciate differences and to resolve our problems without anxiety and frustration. There are a finite number of nuclear warheads, but there are an infinite number of positive ideas and projects and an infinite amount of energy for the crew members of this planet to create the world we envision.

Look at the food issue. The crisis in Africa proved to be an excellent opportunity to deepen global connectedness. In 1984–85, as a result of programs like "Band-Aid," "We Are the World," and "Live-Aid," individuals around the world pulled together and contributed over $150 million to support our hungry crew members during the African food crisis. These were individuals, not governments. Anyone with commitment can make a difference. The schoolchildren of New York City, many from poor ghetto areas, put aside their nickels and dimes, and raised money from other sources, hired their own Boeing 747, and shipped $150,000 worth of grain directly to the hungry in Ethiopia. They did all of this within a period of a few months. I was deeply moved when I saw a video of kids in New York watching a video of their fellow children in Ethiopia eating the food that the New Yorkers had provided with their own lunch money. Television was put to good use, allowing children to experience fully the fruits of their labor.

Humanity's ability to respond with increased speed and effectiveness to major crises is evidence of our evolutionary shift toward greater global connectedness. In the issue of famine, we have responded more quickly with each decade, from Bangladesh in the sixties, the Sahel drought and Cambodia in the seventies, Somalia in the early eighties, to Ethiopia in 1985. Through technology we are linked up within minutes to any place on the planet. We have indeed become neighbors in a global village, even though most people are as yet unaware of it.

We're not just throwing money at problems. Whole nations are discovering their ability to cocreate their own solutions, thus raising their levels of self-sustainability. In 1985, Zimbabwe was able to feed all its people, store half a million tons of grain for the future, and export half a million tons to hungry people in the rest of Africa. There are artifacts everywhere of increased food production—such as the Windstar Biodome[56]—which demonstrate that you can produce food efficiently in abundance in marginal food-growing areas.

Remember when most people gave China up for lost in the 1950s because of their incredible population growth and food production problems? Today, China is one of the most self-sustaining countries on the planet. As of 1985, they have 22% of the world's population and they consume 22% of the world's food. Basically, the severe hunger and population problems have been resolved.

The country of Sri Lanka, with a totally different politico-economic structure, was considered another lost cause. They also solved the problem of hunger and self-sustainability.

There's good news about energy too. By 1979, people in the United States were painfully aware that we had an energy problem. In the following five years, the U.S. obtained more than a hundred times more energy from efficiency, conservation, and improvements than from the net combination of nuclear, oil, and coal expansions.[57] The analogy is a simple one: Instead of continually pouring more water into a leaking bucket, we can save enormous amounts of money and energy by plugging the holes. Our willingness to change proved far more effective than repeating old unworkable patterns.

Sweden has also paved the way to doing even more with less. In 1985, Sweden had the same standard of living as the United States but consumed only half the amount of energy per capita.

It all starts with people—their visions and their commitment to action, to do whatever it takes. A thousand-mile trek begins with a single step. As Edmund Burke said, "No one made a bigger mistake than he who did nothing because he could do only a little."

It's about people. You and me. Citizen diplomacy does work. Soviet and U.S. schoolchildren are exchanging letters and visits. Cities are adopting sister cities. The astronaut-cosmonaut program promotes cooperation in space. In 1986, world-famous pianist Vladimir Horowitz, who defected to the U.S. as a young man, was invited back to Moscow to perform for his countrymen. Both Soviets and Americans rejoiced in the reunion. And at the Goodwill Games, first held in the summer of 1986 and planned as an annual event, athletes convened to promote goodwill through sports.

All of this is happening because people are responding to a deeper bond with each other and the planet and are choosing to take action. Robert Muller, former assistant secretary general of the United Nations, has passionately stated:

Use every letter you write
Every conversation you have
Every meeting you attend
To express your fundamental beliefs and dreams
Affirm to others the vision of the world you want
You are a free, immensely powerful source
of life and goodness
Affirm it
Spread it
Radiate it
Think day and night about it
And you will see a miracle happen:
the greatness of your own life.[58]

Even one, seemingly tiny action can make all the difference.

> *"Tell me the weight of a snowflake," a coal-mouse [a small bird] asked a wild dove.*
>
> *"Nothing more than nothing," was the answer.*
>
> *"In that case, I must tell you a marvelous story," the coal-mouse said.*
>
> *"I sat on the branch of a fir, close to its trunk, when it began to snow— not heavily, not in a raging blizzard—no, just like in a dream, without a wind, without any violence. Since I did not have anything better to do, I counted the snowflakes settling on the twigs and needles of my branch. Their number was exactly 3,741,952. When the 3,741,953rd dropped onto the branch, nothing more than nothing as you say, the branch broke off."*
>
> *Having said that, the coal-mouse flew away.*
>
> *The dove, since Noah's time an authority on the matter, thought about the story for a while, and finally said to herself, "Perhaps there is only one person's voice lacking for peace to come to the world."*[59]

It all comes back to you—the individual. To truly have good news, you must *be* good news. The Aiki Approach is a powerful tool for bringing forth your vision of the world. When your life is a contribution, a source of value to the world, you are living beyond the gold, beyond success. The only limit to how far you can go is in your willingness to leap into the unknown.

Reconsider the question I posed in the first chapter: What would it be like if you lived each day, each breath, as a work of art in progress? Imagine that you are a masterpiece unfolding, every second of every day, now and now and now and now. A work of art taking form with each breath. What would it be like if you lived that life?

It is a quality of being, not just a quantity of doing. It is beyond success. In a life of artistry, even the *quantity* of our work far surpasses that of the frenzied, busy approach. We don't just make the news, we are the news.

Gandhi sat for weeks in meditation, much to the discomfort of those around him, when he needed to decide on what to do about the salt tax and about Indian-British relations. To the constant pleading of "What have you decided?" his reply was, "I have not decided anything yet. The answer will be here. It's not here yet."

When it became clear, he acted simply, powerfully, and effectively. He made an historic walk to the sea, and with a single grasp of his hand, he picked up a handful of salt from nature, from his own India, and declared that salt was free. Thus he changed the entire course of Indian history. When you have clarity of vision, from that centered, heartfelt space, the proper direction and path will emerge naturally and powerfully.

As we integrate the Aiki Approach into our daily life, we develop the delicate balance of taking full responsibility for our lives and at the same time letting go of the unnecessary stress and busy-ness that often come from a committed and passionate life. It is this unique combination of going for it and letting go, taking responsibility and trusting, that takes us beyond success.

By choosing this extraordinary state called artistry, we experience heightened awareness and a deeper connectedness to our world. We go beyond the gold, but more than that, we discover that we *are* the gold that brings joy and fulfillment to the world. What looks like the end is just the beginning.

May your life of work become a work of art.


*It is no use walking anywhere to preach unless our walking is our preaching.*
St. Francis of Assisi

# NOTES

1. "My Speech to the Graduates," in *Side Effects*, by Woody Allen (Random House, 1980).
2. Best known for the invention of the geodesic dome, Buckminster Fuller dreamed and dared to be different. "Bucky," as he was known by all, emerged from expulsion from Harvard, severe alcoholism, and flirtations with suicide to become an inventor, architect, mathematician, engineer, philosopher, and poet. Bucky held twenty-six patents, wrote twenty-four books, and received an equal number of honorary degrees. Bucky created the Dymaxion concept, which resulted in a superfast, fuel-efficient, three-wheeled car in 1933, and a map that first showed all Earth's continents without distortion. During the 1960s, he popularized the term "Spaceship Earth" and was the first to write of the problems of a closed-system planet. In 1969, he was nominated for the Nobel Peace Prize. Marshall McLuhan called him "the Leonardo da Vinci of our time."
3. "Aikido and the New Warrior," by Bob Aubrey, in *Aikido and the New Warrior*, edited by Richard Strozzi Heckler (North Atlantic Books, 1985).
4. *Great Lives, Great Deeds* (The Reader's Digest Association, 1964).
5. *A Will Rogers Treasury*, by Bryan B. and Frances N. Sterling (Crown Publishers, 1982).
6. *Free to Be Muhammad Ali*, by Robert Lipsyte (Harper & Row, 1978).
7. See note 6 above.
8. *100 Ways to Enhance Self Concepts in the Classroom*, by Jack Canfield and Harold Wells (Prentice-Hall, 1976).
9. "On Space," by Rusty Schweickart, Transcript of the First Annual Windstar Choices for the Future Symposium, Snowmass, Colorado, June 1986.
10. "Federal Express' Fred Smith," interview by Robert B. Tucker, in *Inc.*, October 1986.
11. *Ki* development exercises have been a part of certain aikido styles for many years. I learned this exercise (and many others, including the centering exercise in Chapter 4) from Rod Kobayashi of Los Angeles and Koichi Tohei of Tokyo. Koichi Tohei's book *Ki in Daily Life* is an excellent reference for *ki* development exercises.
12. *The Lazy Man's Guide to Enlightenment*, by Thaddeus Goles (Bantam, 1980), is a wonderful treatise on the contraction and expansion theory of relationships.
13. A more intensive explanation of breathing and *ki* development can be found in *Ki In Daily Life*, by Koichi Tohei (Harper & Row, 1978)
14. See note 4 above.
15. See note 4 above.
16. *Winning Life's Toughest Battles*, by Dr. Julius Segal (McGraw-Hill Book Co., 1986).
17. *Mark Twain: An American Voice*, by Patricia Dendtler Frevert (Creative Education, Inc., 1981).
18. "The Founder, Ueshiba Morihei," by John Stevens, in *Aikido and the New Warrior*, edited by

Richard Strozzi Heckler (North Atlantic Books, 1985).

19. An excellent book that led me to consider the nature of belief systems and violence is *The Passionate Mind* by Joel Kramer (Celestial Arts, 1974).

20. This box was based on work done by Jack Zwissig, trainer for Lifespring in Los Angeles.

21. "Self-esteem," by Jack Canfield (audio cassette tape, 1985).

22. See note 2 above.

23. "The View From the Year 2000," by Barry Farrell, in *Life Magazine*, February 26, 1971.

24. See note 23 above.

25. *Critical Path*, by R. Buckminster Fuller (St. Martin's Press, 1981).

26. Morihei Ueshiba, the founder of aikido, used the symbol below in communicating aikido.  Aikido instructor Terry Dobson and Victor Miller, in their book *Giving In To Get Your Way* (Delacorte Press, 1978), effectively use circles, squares, and triangles as a way to communicate the forms of conflict and one's reactions to them. A more detailed development of the use of geometry in conflict situations can be found in their book.

27. *Getting to Yes*, by Roger Fisher and William Ury (Houghton Mifflin, 1981).

28. See note 27 above.

29. See note 4 above.

30. See note 4 above.

31. "He Won't Walk Again," in *Challenged by Handicap*, by Richard B. Lyttle (Reilly & Lee, 1971).

32. *Born to Win*, by John Bertrand (Hearst Marine Books, 1985).

33. See note 27 above.

34. *Hearts That We Broke Long Ago*, by Merle Shain (Bantam, 1985).

35. *Giving In To Get Your Way*, by Terry Dobson and Victor Miller (Delacorte Press, 1978).

36. "Ebony and Ivory," by Jeannie Ralston, in *McCall's*, October 1986.

37. Tim Gallwey, author of *The Inner Game of Tennis* and *The Inner Game of Golf*, conducts workshops around the country on his unique learning theories.

38. "How to Succeed Without Even Vying," by Alfie Kohn, in *Psychology Today*, September 1986.

39. "Excerpts from the Writings and Transcribed Lectures of the Founder," in *Aiki News*, January 1983.

40. This exercise was based on work done by Russell Bishop, founder of "Insight," located in Santa Monica, California.

41. "21 Kids Who Have Made a Difference," by Anne Cassidy and the Articles Department Staff, in *McCall's*, July 1986.

42. *How Can I Help*, by Ram Dass and Paul Gorman (Alfred A. Knopf, 1985).

43. See note 26 above.

44. How Community Boards work is perhaps best explained from the standpoint of what has not seemed to work in the past. In 1976, Ray Shonholtz, a former Monterey public defender and then professor of law at the University of San Francisco, was convinced that the criminal justice system is called upon after disputes have escalated to the violent level and that certain conflicts could be resolved in the neighborhoods and outside the court system, before violence erupted. Out of this conviction, the Community Board program was born. The program now operates in several cities in the United States, both in neighborhoods and school systems. For more information on this unique program, contact Community Board Center for Policy and Training, 149 Ninth St., San Francisco, CA 94103.

45. *Open Mind, Whole Mind*, by Bob Samples (Addison-Wesley, 1987).

46. Statistics for food consumption were calculated from production statistics taken from the United Nations Food and Agriculture Organization 1984 Production Year Book, adjusted by trade figures from the 1984 United Nations Trade Year Book and aid figures from the Food and Agriculture Organization's "Food Aid in Figures."

47. The energy information is taken from the 1984 United Nations Energy Statistics Year Book.

48. "How Not To Parachute More Cats," by Amory and Hunter Lovins, in *The Windstar Journal*, Fall 1986.

49. See note 3 above.

50. Peter Bourne is a physician and anthropologist who has been involved in international health and development issues for the last fifteen years, with experience in more than forty developing countries. He served as assistant secretary general at the United Nations and as Special Assistant to the President for Health Affairs in the Carter White House. In addition to his work at Global Water, he is on the board of directors of the Global Hunger Project.

51. "World Military and Social Expenditures, 1985," by Ruth Leger Sivard (World Priorities, Inc., 1985).

52. "On Hunger," by Peter Bourne, Transcript of the First Annual Windstar Choices for the Future Symposium, Snowmass, Colorado, June 1986.

53. "Profiles," *The New Yorker* magazine, March 4, 1985.
54. See note 53 above.
55. Statistic is from the Center for Defense Information in Washington, D.C.
56. Windstar's Biodome project is a major effort to employ design in the service of nature instead of imposing technology on nature. The basic design is spun off from the work of Buckminster Fuller. On a small area of land, a high-density growing environment is created that conserves energy, soil, and water and recycles nutrients between the horticultural and aquacultural systems. Vegetables, fruits, and fish are produced in a Mediterranean-like climate regardless of the outdoor weather conditions. A twenty-five-foot diameter prototype dome has been in operation on the Windstar land since the summer of 1984. By observing the operation and performance of the small dome, new design ideas have been integrated into the fifty-foot diameter Biodome now under construction at Windstar. A pilot project concept has been established whereby ten Biodomes will be placed in different climates to evaluate how the design can be further refined to provide a healthy growing environment in a wide range of climates. The first of these pilot Biodomes went into operation on a farm community in Waynesville, North Carolina, in October of 1986. For more information on the Biodome project, contact John Katzenberger, Design Director, The Windstar Foundation, Box 178, Snowmass, Colorado 81654.
57. See note 48 above.
58. "On Peace," by Robert Muller, Transcript of the First Annual Windstar Choices for the Future Symposium, Snowmass, Colorado, June 1986.
59. "A Tale for all Seasons," *New Fables: Thus Spoke "The Carabou,"* by Kurt Kauter.

# ABOUT THE AUTHOR

Thomas Crum arrived in 1945 at the dawn of the atomic age. Graduating from college in the tumultuous sixties with a Bachelor of Science degree in mathematics and a secondary school teaching certificate, he entered the multinational corporate world in the area of systems analysis and sales. In the early 1970s he taught at and directed the Aspen Community School, an exemplary humanistic school for children grades K–8.

A multisport athlete throughout his life, he has continued to work with a wide variety of athletes, both amateur and professional, in breakthrough performance principles and increasing mind-and-body coordination and efficiency. Currently he is conducting special Ski Aiki programs with the Aspen Skiing Company.

Thomas is cofounder and former executive director of the Aspen Academy of Martial and Healing Arts, and was chief instructor in the art of aikido. For over two decades he has been involved in the martial arts, from western boxing and wrestling to various arts from Japan, China, Korea, and the Philippines.

Thomas is cofounder, with John Denver, and former executive director of the Windstar Foundation, an international education and research center on creating a sustainable and prosperous future. He is founder and president of Aiki Works, Inc. and is presently spending his time living, developing, and communicating the Aiki Approach to Living through writing, audio and video tapes, and seminars.

# AIKI WORKS, INC.

AIKI WORKS, INC., an educational corporation founded by Thomas Crum in 1985, is dedicated to bringing the harmonizing Aiki Approach and mind/body integration principles to individuals and organizations to enhance performance in conflict resolution, stress management, team building, and breakthrough performance. AIKI WORKS, INC., addresses these and other subjects in print, on audio and video tape, and on film.

Thomas Crum and his staff are available to present a variety of programs ranging in scope from keynote addresses to weeklong workshops. Seminars and workshops are tailored to meet the individual needs of corporations, professional associations, educational institutions, and the general public. The Aiki Approach is offered as an inhouse program or residency program in Aspen, Colorado. In addition, special in-the-field programs are held combining this work in a retreat/play atmosphere of downhill skiing and winter mountaineering.

For complete information on seminars and products, contact:

AIKI WORKS, INC.
BOX 7845
ASPEN, COLORADO 81612
303/925-7099